PREJUDICES
FOURTH SERIES

PREJUDICES
FOURTH SERIES
By H. L. MENCKEN

OCTAGON BOOKS

A DIVISION OF FARRAR, STRAUS AND GIROUX

New York   1977

Copyright 1924 by Alfred A. Knopf, Inc.
Copyright renewed 1952 by H. L. Mencken

Reprinted 1977
by special arrangement with Alfred A. Knopf, Inc.

OCTAGON BOOKS
A DIVISION OF FARRAR, STRAUS & GIROUX, INC.
19 Union Square West
New York, N.Y. 10003

Library of Congress Cataloging in Publication Data

Mencken, Henry Louis, 1880-1956.
  Prejudices: fourth series.

  Reprint of the ed. published by Knopf, New York.
  Includes index.
  I. Title.

| PS3525.E43P84 1977 | 818′.5′209 | 76-54781 |
| ISBN 0-374-95577-8 | | |

Manufactured by Braun-Brumfield, Inc.
Ann Arbor, Michigan
Printed in the United States of America

CONTENTS

CONTENTS

CONTENTS

PREJUDICES
FOURTH SERIES

PREJUDICES: FOURTH SERIES

I. THE AMERICAN TRADITION

1

EVER since Dr. William Crary Brownell, *de l'Académie Américaine*, published his little volume, "Standards," in 1917, a vast hullabaloo has been going on among the native, white, Protestant *Gelehrte* of the Republic, particularly in the great open spaces of the South and Middle West, in favor of what they call the American tradition in letters. Perhaps I libel Brownell, a worthy if somewhat gummy man, by hinting that he started this whooping; it may be that its actual generator was George Creel, the Rev. Dr. Newell Dwight Hillis, the Hon. James M. Beck, the Hon. A. Mitchell Palmer or some other such master-mind of that patriotic and intelligent era. Whatever its parentage, it was at least born in the holiest of wedlock, and to the applause of all right-thinking men; and if I now presume to pull its ear I surely hope that no one will suspect that I thereby question its legitimacy. It is, in fact, absolutely and irrefragably American from snout to *os calcis*, not only in outward seeming and demeanor, but also in inner essence, and anyone who flouts it also flouts everything that is most sacred in the spirit of Americanism.   To that business I herewith address myself briefly.

What, then, is the spirit of Americanism?   I precipitate it conveniently into the doctrine that the way to ascertain the truth about anything, whether in the realms of exact knowledge, in the purple zone of the fine arts or in the empyrean reaches of metaphysics, is to take a vote upon it, and that the way to propagate that truth, once it has been ascertained and proclaimed by lawful authority, is with a club.   This doctrine, it seems to me, explains almost everything that is indubitably American, and particularly everything American that is most puzzling to men of older and less inspired cultures, from American politics to American learning, and from the lush and unprecedented American code of morals to the amazing and almost fabulous American code of honor.   At one end it explains the archetypical buffooneries of the Ku Klux Klan, the American Legion, the Anti-Saloon League, the Department of Justice and all other such great engines of cultural propaganda, and at the other end it explains the amusing theory that the limits of the nation's æsthetic adventures are to be fixed by a vague and self-appointed camorra of rustic Ph.D.'s, and that any artist, indigenous or imported, who dares to pass them is not only a sinner against the beautiful but also a traitor to the flag, and that he ought, shall and must be throttled by the secular arm. Patriotism thus gathers in æsthetics and gives it suck, as it has already given suck to ethics. There are artists who are worthy of the boon of freedom, and there are artists who are criminal and must be put down, as anarchists and polygamists are put down. The fancies of the poet in his velvet coat, the vast soarings and grapplings of the metaphysician in his damp cell, the writhings of the logician chained to his rock, become either right or wrong, and whatever is right in them is American and whatever is wrong is not American.

How far this last notion goes under the Constitution is best shown, not in the relatively *pianissimo* pronunciamentoes of such suave and cautious dons as Brownell, who are themselves often sadly polluted by foreign ideas, despite their heroic struggle to remember Valley Forge and San Juan Hill, but in the far more frank and passionate bulls of their followers in the seminaries of the cow States, where every male of *Homo sapiens* has copious *vibrissæ* on his chest and Nordic blue eyes in his head, and is a red-blooded, go-getting, up-and-coming he-man. I introduce at once a perfect specimen, Doughty of Texas —a savant but little known in the diabetic East, but for long a favorite expert in comparative morals in the university at Austin—not a professor, alas, for he lacks the Ph.D., but *amicus curiæ* to the other professors, as befits his trade of jurisconsult, and a frequent author of critical papers. Doughty has passion but he also has diligence: a combination not too common. Unlike the lean and slippered Beers, of Yale, who once boasted that he had read none of the books he was denouncing, Doughty is at pains to look into even the most subversive, as a dutiful Censor Librorum looks into even "Science and Health" and the works of Dr. Marie C. Stopes. Some time ago, determined to get at and expose the worst, he plowed magnificently through a whole library—through all the new poetry from Carl Sandburg to "The Spoon River Anthology," and all the new novels from Dreiser to Waldo Frank, and all the vast mass of immoral criticism accompanying them, from that in the *Dial* and the *Nation* to that in the *Little Review, S4N* and the Chicago *Literary Times*. "For many months now," he reported when he emerged at last, "there has passed before me the whole ghastly array. . . . I have read the 'books'; the 'fiction' and the 'verse'; the 'drama,' the 'articles' and the 'essays'; the 'sketches' and the 'criticisms,' and whatever else is squeaked and gibbered by these unburied and not-to-be-handled dead. . . . It is this unnamable by-product of congenital deficiency,

perverted dissipation and adulterated narcotics
. . . which I refer to as 'modern [American] literature.' "

And what is the Texas Taine's verdict upon this
modern American literature? The verdict, in brief,
of all other right-thinking, forward-looking he-men,
North, East, South, West—the verdict of every American who truly loves the flag, and knows congenitally
what is right and what is wrong. He not only finds
that it is, in itself, nothing but "swept-up rottenness
and garbage—the dilute sewage of the sordid mental
slums of New York and Chicago"; he also finds that
the ladies and gentlemen who compose it are no more
than "a horde of chancre-laden rats," that they constitute a "devil's crew of perverted drug-addicts,"
that they are engaged unanimously upon a "flabby
and feeble assault . . . upon that ancient decency
that for unnumbered generations of the white North-
ern races of mankind, at least, has grown and
strengthened as a seed cast upon kindly soil," and,
finally, that "no one of the 'writers' of this unhappy
array was in the service of the United States in the
Great War"—in brief, that the whole movement is
no more than a foul conspiracy to tear down the flag,
uproot the Republic and exterminate the Nordic
Blond, and that, in consequence, it is the duty of
every American who is a member "of a white Nordic
race, save the Teutonic," to come sliding down the

pole, grab the tarpot, and go galloping to the alarm. So concluding and stating in rich Texan phrases, the Doughty proceeds to rend specifically a typical book by one of these immigrant foes to "the heritage of American and English men.". . . The one he chooses is "Jurgen," by James Branch Cabell, of Virginia!

2

This long-horned policeman of letters, I admit, is more exuberant than most. There are no soothing elms on the campus at Austin; instead there is only the cindered *plaza de toros* of the Ku Klux Klan. Patriotism, down there, runs wilder than elsewhere. Men have large hands and loud voices. The sight of the flag makes their blood leap and boil; when it is affronted they cannot control themselves. Nevertheless, the doctrine thus stated in harsh terms by the dreadful Doughty, is, in its essence, precisely the doctrine of his more urbane colleagues—of Brownell *de l'Académie Américaine,* of Brander Matthews *de l'Académie Américaine,* of Sherman *de l'Académie Américaine,* of Erskine *de l'Institut National,* of Boynton, of old Beers, of all the rest. It is a doctrine, as I have said, that is thoroughly American—as American, indeed, as Prohibition, correspondence schools, the Knights of Pythias or chewing-gum. But by the same token it is a doctrine that has no more fundamental sense or dignity than the politics of a Coolidge or the theology of a Billy Sunday. It is, to come to the bald fact at once, mere drivel—an endless series of false assumptions and *non-sequiturs*—bad logic piled recklessly upon unsound facts. It is the product of men who, drilled beyond their capacity for taking in ideas and harrowed from infancy by harsh and unyielding concepts of duty, have borrowed the patriotic philosophy of surburban pastors and country schoolmarms, and now seek to apply it to the consideration of phenomena that are essentially beyond their comprehension, as honor is beyond the comprehension of a politician. It is rural Fundamentalism in the black gown and disarming whiskers of *Wissenschaft;* its inevitable fruit is what Ernest Boyd has aptly called Ku Klux Kriticism.

The simple truth, of course, is that the standards and traditions these sublimated Prohibition enforcement officers argue for so eloquently have no actual existence in the first-line literature of the American people—that what they demand is not a lofty fidelity to a genuine ideal, but only an artificial and absurd subservience to notions that were regarded with contempt by every American of the civilized minority even when they prevailed. In other words, what they argue for is not a tradition that would take in Poe, Hawthorne, Emerson, Whitman and Mark Twain, but a tradition that would pass over all these men to embrace Cooper, Bryant, Donald G. Mitchell, N. P. Willis, J. G. Holland, Charles Dudley Warner, Mrs. Sigourney and the Sweet Singer of Michigan. Even Longfellow, I daresay, must be left out, for didn't he drink of green and terrible waters in Paris as a youth and didn't Poe accuse him of stealing from the Spanish and the German? Certainly even Longfellow, to go back to Doughty's interdict, "simmered in the devil's cauldron of central Europe" and was "spewed out of Italy and France." Could Bryant himself qualify? Didn't he trifle with strange tongues and admire enemy aliens? And what of Lowell? His Dante studies surely had a sinister smack; one can't imagine a Texas Grand Goblin approving them. Bayard Taylor I refrain from mentioning at all. His translation of "Faust" came to a just judgment at last when it was hurled from the shelves of every American university patronized by the issue of 100 per cent. Americans. Its incineration on a hundred far-flung campuses, indeed, was the second great patriotic event of the *annus mirabilis* which saw the launching of Brownell's "Standards" and the entrance of the Ku Klux Klan into literary criticism.

How little the patriot-pedagogues know of the veriest elements of American literary history was shown very amusingly some time ago when one of them, a specialist in the Emerson tradition, got himself into a lather denouncing some Greenwich Village Brandes for arguing that beauty was independent of morals and its own sufficient justification—only to be confronted by the disconcerting fact that Emerson himself had argued the same thing. Can it be that even pedagogues are unaware that Emerson came to fame by advocating a general deliverance from the stupid and flabby tradition his name is now evoked to support, that his whole system of ideas was an unqualified protest against hampering traditions of every sort, that if he were alive today he would not be with the professors but unalterably against them? And Emerson was surely not alone. Go through the list of genuinely first-rate men: Poe, Hawthorne, Whitman, Mark Twain. One and all they stood outside the so-called tradition of their time; one and all, they remained outside the tradition that pedants try so vainly to impose upon a literature in active being today. Poe's poems and tales not only seemed strange to the respectable dolts of his time; they seemed downright horrible. His criticism, which tells us even more about him, was still worse: it impinged upon such dull fellows as Griswold exactly as "Jennie Gerhardt" impinged upon the appalled tutors in the alfalfa colleges. And what of Hawthorne? Hawthorne's onslaught upon the Puritan ethic was the most formidable and effective ever delivered, save only Emerson's. And Whitman?

Whitman so staggered the professors that it is only within the last few years that they have begun to teach him at all; those who flourished in 1870 avoided all mention of him as carefully as their successors of today avoid mention of Dreiser or Cabell. And Mark Twain? I put a professor on the stand, to wit, my Christian friend, Phelps of Yale. Go to Phelps' "Essays on Modern Novelists," and you will find a long and humorous account of the efforts of unintelligent pedagogues to read Mark out of the national letters altogether—and go to Van Wyck Brooks' "The Ordeal of Mark Twain" and you will discover what great damage that imbecility did to the man himself. Phelps printed his book in 1910. It was the first book by a doctor of beautiful letters to admit categorically that Mark was an artist at all! All the other professors, even in 1910, were still teaching that Washington Irving was a great humorist and Mark a mere clown, just as they are teaching now that the criticism of Howells and Lowell was superior to the criticism of Huneker, and that Henry van Dyke is a great artist and Cabell a bad one.

Historically, there is thus nothing but folly and ignorance in all the current prattle about a restoration of the ancient American tradition. The ancient American tradition, in so far as it was vital and productive and civilized, was obviously a tradition of individualism and revolt, not of herd-morality and conformity. If one argues otherwise, one must inevitably argue that the great men of the Golden Age were not Emerson, Hawthorne, Poe and Whitman, but Cooper, Irving, Longfellow and Whittier. This nonsense, no doubt, is actually argued in the prairie seminaries; it even has its prophets, perhaps, in backwaters of the East; certainly one finds little in controversion of it in the prevailing text-books. But it remains nonsense all the same. The fact that it has been accepted for years explains the three great disgraces of American letters: the long neglect of Whitman, Melville and Mark Twain. And the fact that it is now challenged actively—that practically all young Americans of any appreciable intelligence now rebel against it—that the most significant sign of the times, in many ways, is the open revolt of the new generation against the teaching of their elders—this fact explains the new vigor that has got into American literature, and its consequent running amok. That running amok, to be sure, is leading to excesses —but so did the running amok of Whitman lead to excesses; so did the timorous running amok of Mark Twain. In order to get the rest of "Leaves of Grass" we must somehow manage to survive "A Woman Waits for Me"; in order to get "Huckleberry Finn" we must swallow the buffooneries of "The Innocents

Abroad." In brief, we must be willing to pay a price for freedom, for no price that is ever asked for it is half the cost of doing without it.

3

It so happens that many of the men and women who have sought to exercise this freedom in our time have been of stocks other than the so-called Anglo-Saxon, either wholly or in part—that they have represented the newer stocks which threaten, not only in the fine arts but in practically all departments of human activity, including even business, to oust the Anglo-Saxon from his old hegemony. The fact, in a day of increasing racial consciousness, has greatly colored the whole controversy and made it extraordinarily bitter. The doctrine gradually set up between 1914 and 1917, and given the full force of law in the latter year, that a citizen of German blood, or suspected of German blood, stood on a plane inferior to that occupied by a citizen of British blood, and had a less valid claim to the equal protection of the Constitution and the laws—this doctrine was extended, in the post-war years of terror, to all Americans not specifically Anglo-Saxon. How seriously it has been taken in the more remote parts of the Republic is well displayed by the strophes that I have quoted from good Doughty—a gentleman who seems quite

as content to take his anthropology from Madison
Grant and Gertrude Atherton as he is to take his
manners from the cattle-herders of his native steppes.
Even more ludicrous attempts to set up Ku Klux
criteria in letters might be dredged from the writings
of more urbane, and, in theory, more intelligent and
civilized critics—for example, Brander Matthews.
The rancorous animosity that has pursued such men
as Dreiser is certainly not wholly æsthetic, or even
moral; it is, to a very large extent, racial. The man
is obviously not an Anglo-Saxon; *ergo,* there is
something sinister about him, and he must be put
down. The more solid becomes his position as a
man of letters, the more offensive he becomes to the
colonial mind. His crime, indeed, is that he has
made headway—that a new American tradition, dif-
fering radically from the old one that pedagogues
preach, tends to grow up around him—that in European eyes, and even in English eyes, he becomes
more typical of America than any of the literary
Knights of Pythias who are pitted against him. It
thus becomes a matter of self-preservation to dispose of him, and when it turns out to be difficult to
do so by logical means then there is a quick and easy
recourse to evangelistic means.

The effects of this holy war, alas, have differed
greatly from those intended. Far from alarming and
stampeding the non-Anglo-Saxons upon whom it has

been waged, it has actually forced them, despite their differences, into a certain common action, and so made them far more formidable than they were when it began. And far from establishing any superiority in the Anglo-Saxon, it has only spread the suspicion that, for all his pretensions, he must be a very inferior fellow at bottom, else he would not be so eager to call in the mob to help him in a purely literary feud. As one who has stood on the battlements for years, and smelt the powder of every salvo, I can only report that I have come to believe in this inferiority thoroughly, and that it seems to me to be most obvious in those who most vociferously uphold the so-called American tradition. They are, in the main, extremely stupid men, and their onslaughts are seldom supported by any formidable weight of metal. What they ask the rest of us to do, in brief, is simply to come down voluntarily and irrationally to their own cultural level—the level of a class that easily dominated the country when it was a series of frontier settlements, but that has gradually lost leadership as civilization has crept in. The rest of us naturally refuse, and they thereupon try to make acquiescence a patriotic matter, and to alarm the refractory with all sorts of fantastic penalties. But it must be obvious that they fail far more often than they succeed —and their failure is a melancholy proof of their intrinsic inferiority. The current of thought in the

United States, at least among the relatively civilized minority, is not actually toward the abject colonialism that they advocate; it is against that colonialism. We are further from sweetness and light today than we ever were before, and we are further from cultural slavery to the harassed and care-worn Motherland. With overwhelming numbers on their side, and every form of external authority, and all the prevailing shibboleths, the spokesmen of Anglo-Saxon domination come to grief every time they tackle the minority, or even any minority within the minority, and at no time do they come to grief more dramatically than when they prepare for battle, in the traditional Anglo-Saxon manner, by first trying to tie their opponents' hands.

When I speak of Anglo-Saxons, of course, I speak inexactly and in the common phrase. Even within the bounds of that phrase the American of the prevailing stock is Anglo-Saxon only partially, for there is probably just as much Celtic blood in his veins as Germanic, and his norm is to be found, not South of the Tyne and west of the Severn, but on the bleak Scotch hills. Among the first English colonists there were unquestionably many men of purely Teutonic stock from the East and South of England, and their influence is yet visible in many characteristic American folkways, in certain traditional American ideas —some of them now surviving only in national hy-

pocrisies—, and, above all, in the fundamental pe-
culiarities of the American dialect of English. But
their Teutonic blood was early diluted by Celtic
strains from Scotland, from the North of Ireland and
from the West of England, and today those Americans who are regarded as being most thoroughly
Anglo-Saxons—for example, the mountaineers of the
Appalachian slopes from Vermont to Georgia—are
obviously far more Celtic than Teutonic, not only
physically but also mentally. They are leaner and
taller than the true English, and far more given
to moral obsessions and religious fanaticism. A
Methodist revival is not an English phenomenon; it
is Scotch. So, fundamentally, is Prohibition. So is
the American tendency, marked by every foreign student of our history, to turn all political combats into
moral crusades. The English themselves, of course,
have been greatly polluted by Scotch, Irish and
Welsh blood during the past three centuries, and for
years past their government has been largely in the
hands of Celts, but though this fact, by making them
more like Americans, has tended to conceal the difference that I am discussing, it has certainly not
sufficed to obliterate it altogether. Such a man as
Lloyd George, in all his ways of thinking, is almost
precisely like an American—but the English notion
of humor remains different from the American notion, and so does the English view of personal liberty,

and on the same level of primary ideas there are many other obvious differences.

But though I am thus convinced that the American Anglo-Saxon wears a false label, and grossly libels both of the great races from which he claims descent, I can imagine no good coming of trying to change it. Let him call himself whatever he pleases. Whatever he calls himself, it must be plain that the term he uses designates a genuinely distinct and differentiated race—that he is separated definitely, in character and habits of thought, from the men of all other recognizable strains—that he represents, among the peoples of the earth, almost a special species, and that he runs true to type. There is, indeed, very little tendency to variation in him—that is, in the mass. The traits that he developed when the first mixture of races took place in colonial days are the traits that he still shows; despite the vast changes in his material environment, he is almost precisely the same, in the way he thinks and acts, as his forefathers were. Some of the other great races of men, during the past two centuries, have changed very noticeably—for example, think of the complete dying out of adventurousness in the Spaniards and its sudden appearance in the Germans—but the American Anglo-Saxon has stuck to his hereditary guns. Moreover, he tends to show much less variation than other races between man and man. It is an axiom that, when five Rus-

sians or Germans meet, there are four parties in conflict, but it is equally an axiom that, among a hundred Americans, at least ninety-five will be found to
hold exactly the same views upon all subjects that
they can grasp at all, and may be trusted to react
exactly alike to all ordinary stimuli.   No other race,
save it be the Chinese, is so thoroughly solid, or so
firmly unresponsive to ideas from without.

4

The good qualities of this so-called Anglo-Saxon
are many, and I am certainly not disposed to question them, but I here pass them over without apology,
for he devotes practically the whole of his literature and fully a half of his oral discourse to cele-
brating them himself, and so there is no danger that
they will ever be disregarded.   No other known man,
indeed, is so violently the blowhard, save it be his
English kinsman; even the Frenchman, by comparison, is relatively modest and reticent.   In this fact
lies the first cause of the ridiculous figure he commonly cuts in the eyes of other people: he brags and
blusters so incessantly that, if he actually had the
combined virtues of Socrates, the Cid and the Twelve
Apostles, he would still go beyond the facts, and so
appear a mere Bombastes Furioso.   This habit, I believe, is fundamentally English, but it has been ex-

aggerated in the Americano by his larger admixture
of Celtic blood. In late years in America it has
taken on an almost pathological character, and is to
be explained, perhaps, only in terms of the Freudian
necromancy. Braggadocio, in the 100 per cent.
American—"we won the war," "it is our duty to lead
the world," "the land of the free and the home of the
brave," the "Americanization" movement, and so on
—is probably no more than a protective mechanism
erected to conceal an inescapable sense of inferiority.

That this inferiority is real must be obvious to any
impartial observer. Whenever the Anglo-Saxon,
whether of the English or of the American variety,
comes into sharp conflict with men of other stocks,
he tends to be worsted, or, at best, to be forced back
upon extraneous and irrelevant aids to assist him in
the struggle. Here in the United States his defeat is
so palpable that it has filled him with vast alarms,
and reduced him to seeking succor in grotesque and
extravagant devices. In the fine arts, in the sciences
and even in the more complex sorts of business the
children of the later immigrants are running away
from the descendants of the early settlers. To call
the roll of Americans eminent in almost any field of
human endeavor beyond that of mere dull money-
grubbing is to call a list of strange and often out-
landish names; even the panel of Congress presents a
startling example. Of the Americans who have

come into notice during the past fifty years as poets, as novelists, as critics, as painters, as sculptors and in the minor arts, less than half bear Anglo-Saxon names, and in this minority there are few of pure Anglo-Saxon blood. So in the sciences. So in the higher reaches of engineering and technology. So in philosophy and its branches. So even in industry and agriculture. In those areas where the competition between the new and the old blood-streams is most sharp and clear-cut, say in New York, in seaboard New England and in the farming States of the upper Middle West, the defeat of the Anglo-Saxon is overwhelming and unmistakable. Once his predominance everywhere was actual and undisputed; today, even where he remains heavily superior numerically, it is largely sentimental and illusory.

The descendants of the later immigrants tend generally to move upward; the descendants of the first settlers, I believe, tend plainly to move downward, mentally, spiritually and even physically. Civilization is at its lowest mark in the United States precisely in those areas where the Anglo-Saxon still presumes to rule. He runs the whole South—and in the whole South there are not as many first-rate men as in many a single city of the mongrel North. Wherever he is still firmly in the saddle, there Ku Kluxery flourishes, and Fundamentalism, and lynching, and Prohibition, and all the other stupid and anti-social crazes of inferior men. It is not in the big cities, with their mixed population, that the death-rate is highest, and politics most corrupt, and religion nearest to voodooism, and every decent human aspiration suspect; it is in the areas that the recent immigrations have not penetrated, where "the purest Anglo-Saxon blood in the world" still flows. I could pile up evidences, but they are not necessary. The fact is too plain to be challenged. One testimony will be sufficient: it comes from two inquirers who made an exhaustive survey of a region in Southeastern Ohio, where "the people are more purely Americans than in the rest of the State":

Here gross superstition exercises strong control over the thought and action of a large proportion of the people. Syphilitic and other venereal diseases are common and increasing over whole counties, while in some communities nearly every family is afflicted with inherited or infectious disease. Many cases of incest are known; inbreeding is rife. Imbeciles, feeble-minded, and delinquents are numerous, politics is corrupt, and selling of votes is common, petty crimes abound, the schools have been badly managed and poorly attended. Cases of rape, assault, and robbery are of almost weekly occurrence within five minutes walk of the corporation limits of one of the county seats, while in another county political control is held by a self-confessed criminal. Alcoholic intemperance is excessive. Gross immorality and its evil results are by no means confined to the hill districts, but are extreme also in the towns.

As I say, the American of the old stock is not unaware of this steady, and, of late, somewhat rapid
degeneration—this gradual loss of his old mastery
in the land his ancestors wrung from the Indian and
the wild cat. He senses it, indeed, very painfully,
and, as if in despair of arresting it in fact, makes
desperate efforts to dispose of it by denial and
concealment. These efforts often take grotesque
and extravagant forms. Laws are passed to hobble
and cage the citizen of newer stocks in a hundred
fantastic ways. It is made difficult and socially
dangerous for him to teach his children the speech
of his fathers, or to maintain the cultural attitudes that he has inherited from them. Every
divergence from the norm of the low-cast Anglo-
Saxon is treated as an *attentat* against the commonwealth, and punished with eager ferocity. On
the level of the country Ku Kluxers the thing goes
to the length of downright assault; a man in Arkansas
or Mississippi who ventured to speak a foreign language, or to concern himself publicly with such of
the fine arts as country Methodists cannot comprehend, or to let it be known that he was a member
of the Roman Catholic Church would run some risk
of being tarred and feathered by his neighbors, or of
having his house burned down over his head. Worse,
there is scarcely less pressure in the higher reaches

of the so-called intellect. The demand for a restoration of what is called the American tradition in letters is nothing more or less, at bottom, than a demand for a supine and nonsensical conformity—a demand that every American, regardless of his racial character and his natural way of thinking, force all his thoughts into the low-caste Anglo-Saxon mold. It is bound to fail of effect, of course, and in that very fact lies the best of imaginable proofs of the mental poverty of those who voice it. It is not brought forward in an effort at persuasion; it is issued as an order, raucously and absurdly—and every time it is flouted the Anglo-Saxon slips another inch down the hill. He cannot prevail in fair competition, and, for all his bellicose flourishes, he cannot prevail by force and intimidation. There remains for him the rôle of martyr, and in this he already begins to display himself affectingly. The music of Americans, we are told gravely, is barred out of our concert halls and opera houses because their managers and conductors are all accursed foreigners. American painters and sculptors have to struggle against a dense tide of immigrants. American criticism has become so anti-American that poets and novelists of the old stock are on a sort of blacklist, and cannot get justice. Only in the colleges does the Anglo-Saxon intellectual hold his own, and even there he is now menaced by swarms of Jews, and must devise means of putting them down or perish with his brothers of the fine arts.

5

It so happens that I am myself an Anglo-Saxon— one of far purer blood, indeed, than any of the half-bleached Celts who pass under the name in the United States and England. I am Angle and I am Saxon, and I am very little else, and that little is all safely white, Nordic, Protestant and blond. Thus I feel free, without risk of venturing into bad taste, to regard frankly the *soi-disant* Anglo-Saxon of this incomparable Republic and his rather less dubious cousin of the Motherland. How do the two appear to me, after a quarter of a century spent largely in accumulating their disfavor? What are the characters that I discern most clearly in the so-called Anglo-Saxon type of man? I may answer at once that two stick out above all others.' One is his curious and apparently incurable incompetence—his congenital inability to do any difficult thing easily and well, whether it be isolating a bacillus or writing a sonata. The other is his astounding susceptibility to fears and alarms—in short, his hereditary cowardice.

To accuse so enterprising and successful a race of

cowardice, of course, is to risk immediate derision; nevertheless, I believe that a fair-minded examination of its history will bear me out. Nine-tenths of the great feats of derring-do that its sucklings are taught to venerate in school—that is, its feats as a race, not the isolated exploits of its extraordinary individuals, most of them at least partly of other stocks—have been wholly lacking in even the most elementary gallantry. Consider, for example, the events attending the extension of the two great empires, English and American. Did either movement evoke any genuine courage and resolution? The answer is plainly no. Both empires were built up primarily by swindling and butchering unarmed savages, and after that by robbing weak and friendless nations: Mexico, Spain, the Boer republics. Neither produced a hero above the average run of those in the movies; neither exposed the folks at home to the slightest danger of reprisal. The battles of Omdurman and Manila Bay were typical of these great swarmings of the Anglo-Saxon—the first a bald massacre, and the second a combat at odds of at least fifty to one. They produced highly typical Anglo-Saxon heroes—Kitchener, an Irishman, and Dewey, largely French. Almost always, indeed, mercenaries have done the Anglo-Saxon's fighting for him—a high testimony to his common sense, but scarcely flattering, I fear, to the truculence he boasts of. The British empire was won mainly by Irishmen, Scotchmen and native allies, and the American empire, at least in large part, by Frenchmen and Spaniards. Moreover, neither great enterprise cost any appreciable amount of blood; neither presented grave and dreadful risks; neither exposed the conqueror to the slightest danger of being made the conquered. The British won most of their vast dominions without having to stand up in a single battle against a civilized and formidable foe, and the Americanos won their continent at the expense of a few dozen puerile skirmishes with savages. All the Indian wars in American history, from the days of John Smith to those of Custer, did not bring down as many men as the single battle of Tannenberg. The total cost of conquering the whole area from Plymouth Rock to the Golden Gate and from Lake George to the Everglades, including even the cost of driving out the French, Dutch, English and Spaniards, was less than the cost of defending Verdun.

So far as I can make out there is no record in history of any Anglo-Saxon nation entering upon any great war without allies, nor upon any war at all when there was the slightest danger of getting beaten, or even of suffering serious damage. The French have done it, the Dutch have done it, the Germans have done it, the Japs have done it, and even such inferior nations as the Danes, the Spaniards, the Boers and the Greeks have done it, but never the English or Americans. Can you imagine the English taking such a chance as the Germans took in 1914, or as the Turks took in 1922, or as the French prepare to take today? Can you imagine the United States resolutely facing a war in which the odds against it were as huge as they were against Spain in 1898? It seems to me that the facts of history are wholly against any such fancy. The Anglo-Saxon always tries to take a gang with him when he goes to war, and even when he has it behind him he is very uneasy, and prone to fall into panic at the first threat of genuine danger. Here I put an unimpeachably Anglo-Saxon witness on the stand, to wit, Dr. Charles W. Eliot, of Harvard. I find him saying, in an article quoted with approbation by the *Congressional Record*, that during the Revolutionary War the colonists now hymned so eloquently in the school-books "fell into a condition of despondency from which nothing but the steadfastness of Washington and the Continental army *and the aid from France* saved them," and that "when the War of 1812 brought grave losses a considerable portion of the population experienced a moral collapse, from which they were rescued only by the exertions of a few thoroughly patriotic statesmen and the exploits of three or four American frigates on the seas"—to say nothing of an enterprising Corsican gentleman, Bonaparte by name.

In both these wars the Americans had enormous and obvious advantages, in terrain, in allies and in men; nevertheless, they fought, in the main, very badly, and from the first shot to the last a majority of them stood in favor of making peace on almost any terms. The Mexican and Spanish Wars I pass over as perhaps too obscenely ungallant to be discussed at all; of the former, General U. S. Grant, who fought in it, said that it was "the most unjust war ever waged by a stronger against a weaker nation." Who remembers that, during the Spanish War, the whole Atlantic Coast trembled in fear of the Spaniards' feeble fleet —that all New England had hysterics every time a strange coal-barge was sighted on the sky-line, that the safe-deposit boxes of Boston were emptied and their contents transferred to Worcester, and that the Navy had to organize a patrol to save the coast towns from depopulation? Perhaps those Reds, atheists and pro-Germans remember it who also remember that during the World War the entire country went wild with fear of an enemy who, without the aid of divine intervention, obviously could not strike it a blow at all—and that the great moral victory was gained at last with the assistance of twenty-one allies and at odds of eight to one.

But the American Civil War remains? Does it, indeed? The almost unanimous opinion of the North, in 1861, was that it would be over after a few small battles; the first soldiers were actually enlisted for but three months. When, later on, it turned unexpectedly into a severe struggle, recruits had to be driven to the front by force, and the only Northerners remaining in favor of going on were Abraham Lincoln, a few ambitious generals and the profiteers. I turn to Dr. Eliot again. "In the closing year of the war," he says, "large portions of the Democratic party in the North *and of the Republican party* advocated surrender to the Confederacy, *so downhearted were they.*" Down-hearted at odds of two to one! The South was plainly more gallant, but even the gallantry of the South was largely illusory. The Confederate leaders, when the war began, adopted at once the traditional Anglo-Saxon device of seeking allies. They tried and expected to get the aid of England, and they actually came very near succeeding. When hopes in that direction began to fade (*i. e.*, when England concluded that tackling the North would be dangerous), the common people of the Confederacy, the progenitors of the chivalric Ku Kluxers of today, threw up the sponge, and so the catastrophe, when it came at last, was mainly internal. The South failed to bring the quaking North to a standstill because, to borrow a phrase that Dr. Eliot uses in another connection, it "experienced a moral collapse of unprecedented depth and duration." The folks at home failed to support the troops in the field, and the troops in the field began to desert. Even so early as Shiloh, indeed, many Confederate regiments were already refusing to fight.

This reluctance for desperate chances and hard odds, so obvious in the military record of the English-speaking nations, is also conspicuous in times of peace. What a man of another and superior stock almost always notices, living among so-called Anglo-Saxons, is (*a*) their incapacity for prevailing in fair rivalry, either in trade, in the fine arts or in what is called learning—in brief, their general incompetence, and (*b*) their invariable effort to make up for this incapacity by putting some inequitable burden upon their rivals, usually by force. The Frenchman, I believe, is the worst of chauvinists, but once he admits a foreigner to his country he at least treats that foreigner fairly, and does not try to penalize him absurdly for his mere foreignness. The Anglo-Saxon American is always trying to do it; his history is a history of recurrent outbreaks of blind rage against peoples who have begun to worst him; hence Know Nothingism, Ku Kluxery, American Legionism, and all the rest of it. Such movements would be inconceivable in an efficient and genuinely self-confident people, wholly assured of their superiority, as a Frenchman is of his or a German of his, and they would be equally inconceivable in a truly gallant and courageous people, disdaining unfair advantages and

overwhelming odds.   Theoretically launched against
some imaginary inferiority in the non-Anglo-Saxon
man, either as patriot, as democrat or as Christian,
they are actually launched at his general superiority,
his greater fitness to survive in the national environment.   The effort is always to penalize him for win-
ning in fair fight, to handicap him in such a manner
that he will sink to the general level of the Anglo-
Saxon population, and, if possible, even below it.
Such devices, of course, never have the countenance
of the Anglo-Saxon minority that is authentically superior, and hence self-confident and tolerant.   Of
that minority I do not speak here.   It is serene in
peace as it is brave in war.   But in the United States,
at least, it is pathetically small, and it tends steadily
to grow smaller and feebler.   The communal laws
and the communal *mores* are made by the folk, and
they offer all the proof that is necessary, not only of
its general inferiority, but also of its alarmed aware-
ness of that inferiority.   The normal American of
the "pure-blooded" majority goes to rest every night
with an uneasy feeling that there is a burglar under
the bed, and he gets up every morning with a sick-
ening fear that his underwear has been stolen.

6

It is difficult, I submit, to admire such a people un-
reservedly, despite the good qualities that I have

passed over. They lack the ease and tolerance, the fine adventurousness and love of hazard which go with a sense of firm security—in other words, with a sense of genuine superiority. The Anglo-Saxon of the great herd is, in many important respects, the least civilized of men and the least capable of true civilization. His political ideas are crude and shallow. He is almost wholly devoid of æsthetic feeling; he does not even make folk-lore or walk in the woods. The most elementary facts about the visible universe alarm him, and incite him to put them down. Educate him, make a professor of him, teach him how to express his soul, and he still remains palpably third-rate. He fears ideas almost more cravenly than he fears men. His blood, I believe, is running thin; perhaps it was not much to boast of at the start; in order that he may exercise any functions above those of a trader, a pedagogue or a mob orator, it needs the stimulus of other and less exhausted strains. Poe, Whitman, Mark Twain—these were typical products of such crosses. The fact that they increase is the best hope of the intellect in America. They shake the old race out of its spiritual lethargy, and introduce it to disquiet and experiment. They make for a free play of ideas. In opposing the process, whether in politics, in letters or in the ages-long struggle toward the truth, the prophets of Anglo-Saxon purity and tradition only make themselves ridiculous. Under the absurd *Kultur* that they advocate Aggasiz would have been deported and Whitman would have been hanged, and the most eminent literati flourishing in the Republic today would be Edgar Guest and Dr. Frank Crane.

The success of these so-called Anglo-Saxons in the world, I am convinced, has been due, not so much to their merits but to their defects—and especially to their high capacity for being alarmed and their aversion to what may be called romance—in other words, to their harshly practical minds, their disdain of intellectual enterprise, their dull common sense. They have saved their hides and their money while better sportsmen were taking chances. But the bitter must go with the sweet. Such qualities belong to *Lumbricus terrestris* rather than to *Homo sapiens.* They may be valuable, but they are not pretty. To-day, at the height of his triumph in the world, the Anglo-Saxon somehow looks shabby—England trembling before one-legged and bankrupt France, the United States engaged in a grotesque *pogrom* against the wop, the coon, the kike, the papist, the Jap, the what-not—worse, engaged in an even more grotesque effort to put down ideas as well as men —to repeal learning by statute, regiment the arts by lynch-law, and give the puerile ethical and theological notions of lonely farmers and corner grocers the force and dignity of constitutional axioms. As

I stand on the side-lines, observing the show, I find it very hard to admire. But, save when ethyl alcohol in dilute aqueous solution has dulled my native pity, I find it even harder to laugh.

II. THE HUSBANDMAN

A READER for years of the *Congressional Record*, I have encountered in its dense and pregnant columns denunciations of almost every human act or idea that is imaginable to political pathology, from adultery to Zionism, and of all classes of men whose crimes the legislative mind can grasp, from atheists to Zoroastrians, but never once, so far as I can recall, has that great journal shown the slightest insolence, direct or indirect, to the humble husbandman, the lonely companion of *Bos taurus*, the sweating and persecuted farmer. He is, on the contrary, the pet above all other pets, the enchantment and delight, the saint and archangel of all the unearthly Sganarelles and Scaramouches who roar in the two houses of Congress. He is more to them, day in and day out, than whole herds of Honest Workingmen, Gallant Jack Tars and Heroic Miners; he is more, even, than a platoon of Unknown Soldiers. There are days when one or another of these totems of the statesman is bathed with such devotion that it would make the Gracchi blush, but there is never a day that the farmer, too, doesn't get his share,

and there is many a day when he gets ten times his
share—when, indeed, he is completely submerged in
rhetorical vaseline, so that it is hard to tell which end
of him is made in the image of God and which is
mere hoof.   No session ever begins without a grand
assault at all arms upon his hereditary foes, from the
boll-weevil and the San José scale to Wall Street and
the Interstate Commerce Commission.   And no session comes to an end without a huge grist of new
laws to save him from them—laws embodying the
most subtle statecraft of the most daring and ingenious body of lawmakers ever assembled under one
roof on the habitable globe.   One might almost
argue that the chief, and perhaps even only aim of
legislation in These States is to succor and secure the
farmer.   If, while the bombs of goose-grease and
rockets of pomade are going off in the two Chambers,
certain evil men meet in the basement and hook
banderillas into him—say, by inserting jokers into
the chemical schedule of a new tariff bill, or by getting the long-haul rules changed, or by manipulating
the loans of the Federal Reserve Banks,—then the
crime is not against him alone; it is against the
whole American people, the common decency of
Christendom, and the Holy Ghost.   Horn a farmer,
and you stand in contumacy to the platforms of all
known parties, to the devout faith of all known states-

men, and to God. *Laborantem agricolam oportet primum de fructibus percipere.*

Paul wrote to the Bishop of Ephesus, at the latest, in the year 65 A. D.; the doctrine that I have thus ascribed to the Mesmers and Grimaldis of our politics is therefore not a novelty of their contrivance. Nor is it, indeed, their monopoly, for it seems to be shared by all Americans who are articulate and devote themselves to political metaphysics and good works. The farmer is praised by all who mention him at all, from archbishops to zoölogists, day in and day out. He is praised for his industry, his frugality, his patriotism, his altruistic passion. He is praised for staying on the farm, for laboriously wringing our bread and meat from the reluctant soil, for renouncing Babylon to guard the horned cattle on the hills. He is praised for his patient fidelity to the oldest of learned professions, and the most honorable, and the most necessary to all of us. He takes on, in political speeches and newspaper editorials, a sort of mystical character. He is no longer a mundane laborer, scratching for the dollar, full of staphylococci, smelling heavily of sweat and dung; he is a high priest in a rustic temple, pouring out his heart's blood upon the altar of Ceres. The farmer, thus depicted, grows heroic, lyrical, pathetic, affecting. To murmur against him becomes a sort of sacrilege, like murmur-

ing against the Constitution, Human Freedom, the
Cause of Democracy. . . . Nevertheless, being already doomed, I herewith and hereby presume to do
it.   More, my murmur is scored in the manner of
Berlioz, for ten thousand trombones *fortissimo,* with
harsh, cacophonous chords for bombardons and
ophicleides in the bass clef.   Let the farmer, so far
as I am concerned, be damned forevermore!   To
hell with him, and bad luck to him!   He is, unless I
err, no hero at all, and no priest, and no altruist, but
simply a tedious fraud and ignoramus, a cheap rogue
and hypocrite, the eternal Jack of the human pack.
He deserves all that he suffers under our economic
system, and more.   Any city man, not insane, who
sheds tears for him is shedding tears of the crocodile.

No more grasping, selfish and dishonest mammal,
indeed, is known to students of the Anthropoidea.
When the going is good for him he robs the rest of us
up to the extreme limit of our endurance; when the
going is bad he comes bawling for help out of the
public till.   Has anyone ever heard of a farmer making any sacrifice of his own interests, however slight,
to the common good?   Has anyone ever heard of a
farmer practising or advocating any political idea
that was not absolutely self-seeking—that was not,
in fact, deliberately designed to loot the rest of us
to his gain?   Greenbackism, free silver, government
guarantee of prices, all the complex fiscal imbecil-

ities of the cow State John Baptists—these are the contributions of the virtuous husbandmen to American political theory. There has never been a time, in good seasons or bad, when his hands were not itching for more; there has never been a time when he was not ready to support any charlatan, however grotesque, who promised to get it for him. Why, indeed, are politicians so polite to him—before election, so romantically amorous? For the plain and simple reason that only one issue ever interests or fetches him, and that is the issue of his own profit. He must be promised something definite and valuable, to be paid to him alone, or he is off after some other mountebank. He simply cannot imagine himself as a citizen of a commonwealth, in duty bound to give as well as take; he can imagine himself only as getting all and giving nothing.

Yet we are asked to venerate this prehensile moron as the *Ur*-burgher, the citizen *par excellence*, the foundation-stone of the state! And why? Because he produces something that all of us must have—that we must get somehow on penalty of death. And how do we get it from him? By submitting helplessly to his unconscionable blackmailing—by paying him, not under any rule of reason, but in proportion to his roguery and incompetence, and hence to the direness of our need. I doubt that the human race, as a whole, would submit to that sort of high-jacking, year in and year out, from any other necessary class of men. When the American railroad workman attempted it, in 1916, there was instant indignation; when a certain small squad of the *Polizei* tried it, a few years later, there was such universal horror that a politician who denounced the crime became President of the United States. But the farmers do it over and over again, without challenge or reprisal, and the only thing that keeps them from reducing us, at intervals, to actual famine is their own imbecile knavery. They are all willing and eager to pillage us by starving us, but they can't do it because they can't resist attempts to swindle each other. Recall, for example, the case of the cotton-growers in the South. They agreed among themselves to cut down the cotton acreage in order to inflate the price—and instantly every party to the agreement began planting *more* cotton in order to profit by the abstinence of his neighbors. That abstinence being wholly imaginary, the price of cotton fell instead of going up— and then the entire pack of scoundrels began demanding assistance from the national treasury—in brief, began demanding that the rest of us indemnify them for the failure of their plot to blackmail us!

The same demand is made almost annually by the wheat farmers of the Middle West. It is the theory of the zanies who perform at Washington that a grower of wheat devotes himself to that banal art in a philanthropic and patriotic spirit—that he plants and harvests his crop in order that the folks of the cities may not go without bread. It is the plain fact that he raises wheat because it takes less labor than any other crop—because it enables him, after working sixty days a year, to loaf the rest of the twelve months. If wheat-raising could be taken out of the hands of such lazy *fellahin* and organized as the production of iron or cement is organized, the price might be reduced by a half, and still leave a large profit for *entrepreneurs*. It vacillates dangerously today, not because speculators manipulate it, but because the crop is irregular and undependable—that is to say, because those who make it are incompetent. The worst speculators, as everyone knows, are the farmers themselves. They hold their wheat as long as they can, borrowing our money from the country banks and hoping prayerfully for a rise. If it goes up, then we pay them an extra and unearned profit. If it goes down, then they demand legislation to prevent it going down next time. Sixty days a year they work; the rest of the time they gamble with our bellies. It is probably the safest gambling ever heard of. Now and then, true enough, a yokel who plunges too heavily comes to grief, and is ingested by the county-town mortgage-shark; now and then a whole county, or State or even larger area goes bankrupt, and the financial dominoes begin falling down

all along the line from Saleratus Center to New York.
But such catastrophes are rare, and they leave no
scars.   When a speculator goes broke in Wall Street
it is a scandalous matter, and if he happens to have
rooked anybody of importance he is railroaded to
jail.   But when a speculator goes broke in the great
open spaces, there is a great rush of political leuco-
cytes to the scene, and presently it is made known that
the sin was not the speculator's at all, but his pro-
jected victims', and that it is the prime duty of the
latter, by lawful order upon the Treasurer of the
United States, to reimburse him his losses and set
him up for a new trial.

The notion that wheat would be much cheaper and
the supply far more dependable if it were grown, not
by a motley horde of such puerile loafers and gam-
blers, but by competent men intelligently organized is
not mine; I borrow it from Henry Ford, a busted
seer.   Since he betrayed them to Dr. Coolidge for a
mess of pottage, the poor Liberals, once so enamored
of his sagacity, denounce Ford as an idiot and a
villain; nevertheless, the fact remains that his discussion of the wastefulness of our present system of
wheat-growing, in the autobiography which he didn't
write, is full of a powerful plausibility.   Ford was
born and brought up on a farm—and it was a farm,
as farms go, ·that was very competently managed.

But he knows very well that even the most competent farmer is but seldom more adept than a chimpanzee playing the violin. The Liberals, indeed, cannot controvert his judgment; they have been thrown back upon belaboring his political morals. What he proposes, they argue, is simply the enslavement of the present farmer, now so gloriously free. With capitalism gradually absorbing his fields, he would have to go to work as a wage-slave. Well, why not? For one, I surely offer no objection. All the rubber we use today is raised by slave labor; so is all the morphine consumed at Hollywood. Our children are taught in school by slaves; our newspapers are edited by slaves. Wheat raised by slave labor would be just as nutritious as wheat raised by men earning $10,000 a year, and a great deal cheaper. If the business showed a good profit, the political clowns at Washington would launch schemes to confiscate it, as they now launch schemes to make good the losses of the farmers. In any case, why bother about the fate of the farmer? If wheat went to $10 a bushel tomorrow, and all the workmen of the cities became slaves in name as well as in fact, no farmer in this grand land of freedom would consent voluntarily to a reduction of as much as $\frac{1}{8}$ of a cent a bushel. "The greatest wolves," says E. W. Howe, another graduate of the farm, "are the farmers who bring produce to town to sell." Wolves? Let us not insult *Canis lupus.* I move the substitution of *Hyæna hyæna.*

Meanwhile, how much truth is in the common theory that the husbandman is harassed and looted by our economic system, that the men of the cities prey upon him—specifically, that he is the chronic victim of such devices as the tariff, railroad regulation, and the banking system? So far as I can make out, there is none whatever. The net effect of our present banking system, as I have already said, is that the money accumulated by the cities is used to finance the farmers, and that they employ it to blackmail the cities. As for the tariff, is it a fact that it damages the farmer, or benefits him? Let us turn for light to the worst Tariff Act ever heard of in human history: that of 1922. It put a duty of 30 cents a bushel on wheat, and so barred out Canadian wheat, and gave the American farmer a vast and unfair advantage. For months running the difference in the price of wheat on the two sides of the American-Canadian border—wheat raised on farms not a mile apart—ran from 25 to 30 cents a bushel. Danish butter was barred out by a duty of 8 cents a pound—and the American farmer pocketed the 8 cents. Potatoes carried a duty of 50 cents a hundredweight—and the potato growers of Maine, eager, as the phrase has it, to mop up, raised such an enormous crop that the market was glutted, and they went bankrupt, and began bawling for government aid. High duties were put, too, upon meats, upon cheese, upon wool—in brief, upon practically everything that the farmer produced. But his profits were taken from him by even higher duties upon manufactured goods, and by high freight rates? Were they, indeed? There was, in fact, no duty at all upon many of the things he consumed. There was no duty, for example, upon shoes. The duty upon woolen goods gave a smaller advantage to the manufacturer than the duty on wool gave to the farmer. So with the duty on cotton goods. Automobiles were cheaper in the United States than anywhere else on earth. So were all agricultural implements. So were groceries. So were fertilizers.

But here I come to the brink of an abyss of statistics, and had better haul up. The enlightened reader is invited to investigate them for himself; they will bring him, I believe, some surprises, particularly if he has been reading the *Congressional Record* and accepting it gravely. They by no means exhaust the case against the consecrated husbandman. I have said that the only political idea he can grasp is one which promises him a direct profit. It is, alas, not quite true: he can also grasp one which has the sole effect of annoying and damaging his enemy, the city man. The same mountebanks who get to Wash·

ington by promising to augment his gains and make good his losses devote whatever time is left over from that enterprise to saddling the rest of us with oppressive and idiotic laws, all hatched on the farm. There, where the cows low through the still night, and the jug of Peruna stands behind the stove, and bathing begins, as at Biarritz, with the vernal equinox— there is the reservoir of all the nonsensical legislation which now makes the United States a buffoon among the great nations.   It was among country Methodists, practitioners of a theology degraded almost to the level of voodooism, that Prohibition was invented, and it was by country Methodists, nine-tenths of them actual followers of the plow, that it was fastened upon the rest of us, to the damage of our bank accounts, our dignity and our ease.   What lies under it, and under all the other crazy enactments of its category, is no more and no less than the yokel's congenital and incurable hatred of the city man—his simian rage against everyone who, as he sees it, is having a better time than he is.

That this malice is at the bottom of Prohibition, and not any altruistic yearning to put down the evils of drink, is shown clearly by the fact that most of the State enforcement acts—and even the Volstead Act, as it is interpreted at Washington—permit the farmer himself to make cider as in the past, and that every effort to deprive him of that astounding im-

munity has met with the opposition of his representatives.   In other words, the thing he is against is not
the use of alcohol *per se*, but simply the use of alcohol in its more charming and romantic forms.   Prohibition, as everyone knows, has not materially
diminished the consumption of alcohol in the cities,
but it has obviously forced the city man to drink
decoctions that he would have spurned in the old
days—that is, it has forced him to drink such dreadful stuff as the farmer has always drunk.   The farmer is thus content with it: it brings his enemy down
to his own level.   The same animus is visible in innumerable other moral statutes, all ardently supported by the peasantry.   For example, the Mann
Act.   The aim of this amazing law, of course, is not
to put down adultery; it is simply to put down that
variety of adultery which is most agreeable.   What
got it upon the books was simply the constant gabble
in the rural newspapers about the byzantine de-
baucheries of urban Antinomians—rich stockbrokers
who frequented Atlantic City from Friday to Monday, vaudeville actors who traveled about the country
with beautiful mistresses, and so on.   Such aphro-
disiacal tales, read beside the kitchen-stove by hinds
condemned to monogamous misery with stupid, un-
clean and ill-natured wives, naturally aroused in
them a vast detestation of errant cockneys, and this
detestation eventually rolled up enough force to at-

tract the attention of the quacks who make laws at Washington. The result was the Mann Act. Since then a number of the cow States have passed Mann Acts of their own, usually forbidding the use of automobiles "for immoral purposes." But there is nowhere a law forbidding the use of barns, cow-stables, hay-ricks and other such familiar rustic ateliers of sin. That is to say, there is nowhere a law forbidding yokels to drag virgins into infamy by the technic practised since Tertiary times on the farms; there are only laws forbidding city youths to do it according to the technic of the great municipalities.

Here we come to the limits of bucolic moral endeavor. It never prohibits acts that are common on the farms; it only prohibits acts that are common in the cities. In many of the Middle Western States there are statutes forbidding the smoking of cigarettes, for cigarette-smoking, to the louts of those wastes, bears the aspect of a citified and levantine vice, and if they attempted it themselves they would be derided by their fellows and perhaps divorced by their wives, just as they would be derided and divorced if they bathed every day, or dressed for dinner, or attempted to play the piano. But chewing tobacco, whether in public or in private, is nowhere forbidden by law, for the plain reason that nine-tenths of all husbandmen practise it, as they practise the drinking of raw corn liquor. The act not only lies within their tastes; it also lies within their means, and hence within their *mores*. As a consequence the inhabitants of the towns in those remote marches are free to chew tobacco all they please, even at divine service, but are clapped into jail the instant they light cigarettes. The same consideration gets into comstockery, which is chiefly supported, like Prohibition, by farmers and chiefly aimed at city men. The Comstock Act is very seldom invoked against newspapers, for the matter printed in newspapers lies within the comprehension of the peasantry, and hence within their sphere of enjoyment. Nor is it often invoked against cheap books of a frankly pornographic character—such things as "Night Life in Chicago," "Adventures on a Pullman Sleeper" and "The Confessions of an ex-Nun"—for when yokels read at all, it is commonly such garbage that they prefer. But they are hot against the infinitely less gross naughtiness of serious books, including the so-called classics, for these books they simply cannot read. In consequence the force of comstockery is chiefly directed against such literature. For one actually vile book that it suppresses it attempts to suppress at least a dozen good ones.

Now the pious husbandman shows signs of an itch to proceed further. Not content with assaulting us with his degraded and abominable ethics, he begins trying to force upon us his still worse theology. On the steppes Methodism has got itself all the estate and dignity of a State religion; it becomes a criminal offense to teach any doctrine in contempt of it.   No civilized man, to be sure, is yet actually in jail for the crime; civilized men simply keep out of such bleak parking spaces for human Fords, as they keep out of Congress and Franz Josef Land.   But the long arm of the Wesleyan revelation now begins to stretch forth toward Nineveh.   The mountebank, Bryan, after years of preying upon the rustics on the promise that he would show them how to loot the cities by wholesale and *à outrance,* now reverses his collar and proposes to lead them in a *jehad* against what remains of American intelligence, already beleagured in a few walled towns.   We are not only to abandon the social customs of civilization at the behest of a rabble of peasants who sleep in their underclothes; we are now to give up all the basic ideas of civilization and adopt the gross superstitions of the same mob.   Is this fanciful?   Is the menace remote, and to be disregarded?   My apologies for suggesting that perhaps you are one of the multitude who thought that way about Prohibition, and only half a dozen years ago.   Bryan is a protean harlequin, and more favored by God than is commonly assumed.   He lost with free silver but he won with Prohibition.   The chances, if my mathematics do not fail, are thus 1 to 1 that he will win, if he keeps his health, with

Fundamentalism—in his own phrase, that God will be put into the Constitution. If he does, then *Eoanthrophus* will triumph finally over *Homo sapiens.* If he does, then the humble swineherd will drive us all into his pen.

Not much gift for Vision is needed to imagine the main outlines of the ensuing *Kultur.* The city man, as now, will bear nine-tenths of the tax burden; the rural total immersionist will make all the laws. With Genesis firmly lodged in the Testament of the Fathers he will be ten times as potent as he is now and a hundred times as assiduous. No constitutional impediment will remain to cripple his moral fancy. The Wesleyan code of Kansas and Mississippi, Vermont and Minnesota will be forced upon all of us by the full military and naval power of the United States. Civilization will gradually become felonious everywhere in the Republic, as it already is in Arkansas. What I sing, I suppose, is a sort of Utopia. But it is not the Utopia of bawdy poets and metaphysicians; it is not the familiar Utopia of the books. It is a Utopia dreamed by simpler and more virtuous men—by seven millions of Christian bumpkins, far-flung in forty-eight sovereign States. They dream it on their long journeys down the twelve billion furrows of their seven million farms, up hill and down dale in the heat of the day. They dream it behind the egg-stove on Winter nights, their boots off and their socks scorching, Holy Writ in their hands. They dream it as they commune with *Bos taurus, Sus scrofa, Mephitis mephitis,* the Methodist pastor, the Ford agent. It floats before their eyes as they scan the Sears-Roebuck catalogue for horse liniment, porous plasters and Bordeaux mixture; it rises before them when they assemble in their Little Bethels to be instructed in the word of God, the plots of the Pope, the crimes of the atheists and Jews; it transfigures the chautauquan who looms before them with his Great Message. This Utopia haunts and tortures them; they long to make it real. They have tried prayer, and it has failed; now they turn to the secular arm. The dung-fork glitters in the sun as the host prepares to march. . . .

Well, these are the sweet-smelling and altruistic agronomists whose sorrows are the *leit-motif* of our politics, whose votes keep us supplied with Bryans and Bleases, whose welfare is alleged to be the chief end of democratic statecraft, whose patriotism is the so-called bulwark of this so-called Republic!

III. HIGH AND GHOSTLY MATTERS

I

The Cosmic Secretariat

THE argument by design, once the bulwark of Christian apologetics, is so full of holes that it is no wonder that it has had to be abandoned. The more, indeed, the theologian seeks to prove the wisdom and omnipotence of God by His works, the more he is dashed by evidences of divine incompetence and stupidity. The world is not actually well run; it is very badly run, and no Huxley was needed to labor the obvious fact. The human body, very adeptly designed in some details, is cruelly and senselessly bungled in other details, and every reflective first-year medical student must notice a hundred ways to improve it. How are we to reconcile this mixture of finesse and blundering with the concept of a single omnipotent Designer, to whom all problems are equally easy? If He could contrive so efficient and durable a machine as the human hand, then how did He come to make such botches as the tonsils, the

gall-bladder, the uterus and the prostate gland?   If
He could perfect the hip joint and the ear, then why
did He boggle the teeth?

Having never encountered a satisfactory—or even
a remotely plausible—answer to such questions, I
have had to go to the trouble of devising one myself.
It is, at all events, quite simple, and in strict accord
with all the known facts.   In brief, it is this: that
the theory that the universe is run by a single God
must be abandoned, and that in place of it we must
set up the theory that it is actually run by a board
of gods, all of equal puissance and authority.   Once
this concept is grasped all the difficulties that have
vexed theologians vanish, and human experience instantly lights up the whole dark scene.   We observe
in everyday life what happens when authority is
divided, and great decisions are reached by consul-
tation and compromise.   We know that the effects at
times, particularly when one of the consultants
runs away with the others, are very good, but we also
know that they are usually extremely bad.   Such a
mixture, precisely, is on display in the cosmos.   It
presents a series of brilliant successes in the midst of
an infinity of failures.

I contend that my theory is the only one ever put
forward that completely accounts for the clinical picture.   Every other theory, facing such facts as sin,
disease and disaster, is forced to admit the supposi-

tion that Omnipotence, after all, may not be omnipotent—a plain absurdity. I need toy with no such nonsense. I may assume that every god belonging to the council which rules the universe is infinitely wise and infinitely powerful, and yet not evade the plain fact that most of the acts of that council are ignorant and foolish. In truth, my assumption that a council exists is tantamount to an *a priori* assumption that its acts are ignorant and foolish, for no act of any conceivable council can be otherwise. Is the human hand perfect, or, at all events, practical and praiseworthy? Then I account for it on the ground that it was designed by some single member of the council—that the business was handed over to him by inadvertence or as a result of an irreconcilable difference of opinion among the others. Had more than one member participated actively in its design it would have been measurably less meritorious than it is, for the sketch offered by the original designer would have been forced to run the gauntlet of criticisms and suggestions from all the other councillors, and human experience teaches us that most of these criticisms and suggestions would have been inferior to the original idea—that many of them, in fact, would have had nothing in them save a petty desire to maul and spoil the original idea.

But do I here accuse the high gods of harboring discreditable human weaknesses? If I do, then my excuse is that it is impossible to imagine them doing the work universally ascribed to them without admitting their possession of such weaknesses. One cannot imagine a god spending weeks and months, and maybe whole geological epochs, laboring over the design of the human kidney without assuming him to have been moved by a powerful impulse to express himself vividly, to marshal and publish his ideas, to win public credit among his fellows—in brief, without assuming him to be egoistic. And one cannot assume him to be egoistic without assuming him to prefer the adoption of his own ideas to the adoption of any other god's. I defy anyone to make the contrary assumption without plunging instantly into clouds of mysticism. Ruling it out, one comes inevitably to the conclusion that the inept management of the universe must be ascribed to clashes of egos, *i. e.*, to petty spites and revenges, among the gods, for any one of them alone, since we must assume him to be infinitely wise and powerful, could run it perfectly. We suffer from bad stomachs simply because the god who first proposed making a stomach aroused thereby the ill-nature of those who had not thought of it, and because they proceeded instantly to wreak that ill-nature upon him by improving, *i. e.*, botching, his work. We must reproduce our species in the familiar arduous, uneconomic, embarrassing and almost pathological manner because the god who devised the excellent process prevailing among the protozoa had to be put in his place when he proposed to extend it to the Primates.

2

The Nature of Faith

Many years ago, when I was more enterprising intellectually than I am to-day, I proposed the application of Haeckel's celebrated biogenetic law—to wit, that the history of the individual rehearses the history of the species—to the domain of human ideas. So applied, it leads to some superficially startling but probably quite sound conclusions, for example, that an adult poet is simply an individual in a state of arrested development—in brief, a sort of moron. Just as all of us, *in utero*, pass through a stage in which we are tadpoles, and almost indistinguishable from the tadpoles which afterward become frogs, so all of us pass through a stage, in our nonage, when we are poets. A youth of seventeen who is not a poet is simply an ass: his development has been arrested even anterior to the stage of the intellectual tadpole. But a man of fifty who still writes poetry is either an unfortunate who has never developed, intellectually, beyond his teens, or a conscious buffoon who pretends to be something that he isn't—

something far younger and jucier than he actually is—, just as the late Richard Mansfield, in Schiller's play, pretended, by the use of a falsetto voice and a girlish skip, to be the eighteen-year-old Don Carlos. Something else, of course, may enter into it. The buffoonery may be partly conscious and deliberate, and partly Freudian. Many an aging man keeps on writing poetry simply because it gives him the illusion that he is still young. For the same reason, perhaps, he plays tennis, wears green cravats, and tries to convince himself that he is in love.

It is my conviction that no normal man ever fell in love, within the ordinary meaning of the term, after the age of thirty. He may, at forty, pursue the female of his species with great assiduity, and he may, at fifty, sixty or even seventy, "woo" and marry a more or less fair one in due form of law, but the impulse that moves him to these follies at such ages is never the complex of illusions and hallucinations that poets describe as love. This complex is quite natural to all males between adolescence and the age of, say, twenty-five, when the kidneys begin to disintegrate. For a youth to reach twenty-one without having fallen in love in an abject and preposterous manner would be for doubts to be raised as to his normalcy. But if he does it after his wisdom teeth are cut, it is no more than a sign that they have been cut in vain—that he is still in his teens, whatever his biological and legal age. Love, so-called, is based upon a view of women that is impossible to any man who has had any experience of them. Such a man may, to the end of his life, enjoy their society vastly, and even respect them and admire them, but, however much he respects and admires them, he nevertheless sees them more or less clearly, and seeing them clearly is fatal to the true romance. Find a man of forty who heaves and moans over a woman in the manner of a poet and you will behold either a man who ceased to develop intellectually at twenty-four or thereabout, or a fraud who has his eye on the lands, tenements and hereditaments of the lady's deceased first husband. Or upon her talents as nurse, cook, amanuensis and audience. This, no doubt, is what George Bernard Shaw meant when he said that every man over forty is a scoundrel.

As I say, my suggestion has not been adopted by psychologists, who, in the main, are a very conservative and unimaginative body of men. If they applied the biogenetic law in the field of religion they might make some interesting observations. The chances are, indeed, that religion belongs exclusively to an extremely early stage of human development, and that its rapid decay in the world since the Reformation is evidence of a very genuine progress. Reduced to its logical essence, every religion now, advocated in Christendom is simply the doctrine that there are higher powers, infinitely wise and virtuous, which take an active interest in the sordid everyday affairs of men, and not infrequently intervene in them. This doctrine is not purely romantic and *a priori;* it is based upon what is regarded by its subscribers as objective evidence. But it must be plain that that evidence tends to go to pieces as human knowledge widens—that it appears massive and impressive in direct proportion as the individual impressed is ignorant. A few hundred years ago practically every phenomenon of nature was ascribed to superhuman intervention. The plague, for example, was caused by God's anger. So was war. So was lightning. Today no enlightened man believes anything of the kind. All these phenomena are seen to be but links in an endless chain of amoral causation, and it is known that, given a certain quite intelligible and usually inevitable combination of causes, they will appear infallibly as effects. Thus religion gradually loses its old objective authority, and becomes more and more a mere sentimentality. An enlightened man's view of it is almost indistinguishable from his view of the Spirit of 1776, the Henty books, and the rosewood casket containing his grandmother's false teeth.

Such a man is not "dead" to religion. He was not born with a congenital inaptitude for it. He has simply outgrown it, as he has outgrown poetry, So-

cialism and love. At adolescence practically all individuals have attacks of piety, but that is only saying
that their powers of perception, at that age, outrun
their knowledge. They observe the phenomenon, but
cannot account for it. Later on, unless their development is arrested, they gradually emerge from
that romantic and spookish fog, just as they emerge
from the hallucinations of secular romance. I speak
here, of course, of individuals genuinely capable of
education—always a small minority. If, as the Army
tests of conscripts showed, nearly 50 per cent. of
American adult males never get beyond the mental development of a twelve-year-old child, then it must be
obvious that a much smaller number get beyond the
mental development of a youth at the end of his
teens. I put that number, at a venture, at 5 per cent.
The remaining 95 per cent. never quite free themselves from religious superstitions. They may no
longer believe it is an act of God every time an individual catches a cold, or sprains his ankle, or cuts
himself shaving, but they are pretty sure to see some
trace of divine intervention in it if he is struck by
lightning, or hanged, or afflicted with leprosy or syphi-
lis. That God causes wars has been believed by all
the Presidents of the United States, save Grover Cleve-
land, since Jefferson's time. During the late war
the then President actually set aside a day for pray-
ing to God to stop what He had started as soon as

possible, and on terms favorable to American investments. This was not done, remember, by a voodoo man in the Congo forest, but by a sound Presbyterian, a Ph.D. of Johns Hopkins University, and the best-dressed professor ever seen at Princeton.

I have said that all modern religions are based, at least on their logical side, on this notion that there are higher powers which observe all the doings of man, and constantly take a hand in them. It should be added that a corollary is almost always appended, to the effect that these higher powers also pronounce ethical judgments upon such human acts as happen to be performed without this intervention, and are themselves animated by a lofty and impeccable morality. Most religions, of course, also embrace a concept of higher powers that are not benign, but malignant—that is, they posit the existence of demons as well as of gods. But there are very few in which the demons are regarded as superior to the gods, or even as their full equals. The great majority of creeds, East and West, savage and so-called civilized, put the gods far above the demons, and teach that the gods always wish the good of man, and that man's virtue and happiness run in direct ratio to his obedience to their desires. That is, they are all based upon the doctrine of what is called the goodness of God. This is true pre-eminently of the chief oriental faiths: Buddhism, Brahminism

and Confucianism. It is true even of Christianity,
despite its luxuriant demonology. No true Christian
can believe that God ever deliberately and wantonly
injures him, or could conceivably wish him ill. The
slings and arrows of God, he believes, are brought
down upon him by his own ignorance and contumacy.
He believes that if he could be like God he would
be perfect.

This doctrine of the goodness of God, it seems to
me, is no more, at bottom, than an evidence of arrested intellectual development. It does not fit into
what we know of the nature and operations of the cosmos today; it is a survival from a day of universal ignorance. That it is still given credit in the Far East is
not surprising, for the intellectual development of the
Far East, despite all the nonsense that is talked about
Indian and Chinese "philosophy," is really no further advanced than that of Europe was in the time
of St. Louis. The most profound Hindoo or Chinese
"philosopher" believes, as objective facts, things that
would make even a Georgia Fundamentalist snicker,
and so his "philosophy" is chiefly worthless, as was
that of the Greeks. The Greeks sometimes guessed
right, just as the swamis and yogis of Los Angeles
sometimes guess right, but in the main their speculations, being based upon false observations, were
valueless, and no one would pay any attention to
them today if it were not for the advertising they get

from theologians, who find them to their taste, and professional "philosophers," who make a living trying to teach them to sophomores. But if the belief in the goodness of God is natural to misinformed orientals, as it was natural to the singularly ignorant Greeks, it is certainly *not* natural to the enlightened races of the West today, for all their science is simply a great massing of proofs that God, if He exists, is neither good nor bad, but simply indifferent—an infinite Force carrying on the operation of unintelligible processes without the slightest regard, either one way or the other, for the comfort, safety and happiness of man.

Why, then, does this belief survive? Largely, I am convinced, because it is supported by another hoary relic from the adolescence of the race, to wit; the weakness for poetry. The Jews fastened their religion upon the Western world, not because it was more reasonable than the religions of their contemporaries—as a matter of fact, it was vastly less reasonable than many of them—, but because it was far more poetical. The poetry in it was what fetched the decaying Romans, and after them the barbarians of the North; not the so-called Christian evidences. For the Jews were poets of a truly colossal eloquence, and they put their fundamental superstitions into dithyrambs of such compelling loveliness that they disarmed the common sense even of skeptical Ro-

mans, and so knocked out all other contemporary
religions, many of which were in far closer accord
with what was then known of the true operations of
the universe. To this day no better poetry has ever
been written. It is so powerful in its effects that
even men who reject its content in toto are more or
less susceptible to it. One hesitates to flout it on
purely æsthetic grounds; however dubious it may be
in doctrine, it is nevertheless almost perfect in form,
and so even the most violent atheist tends to respect
it, just as he respects a beautiful but deadly toad-
stool. For no man, of course, ever quite gets over
poetry. He may seem to have recovered from it,
just as he may seem to have recovered from the
measles of his school-days, but exact observation
teaches us that no such recovery is ever quite perfect;
there always remains a scar, a weakness and a
memory.

Now, there is reason for maintaining that the taste
for poetry, in the process of human development,
marks a stage measurably later than the stage of religion. Savages so little cultured that they know no
more of poetry than a cow have elaborate and often
very ingenious theologies. If this be true, then it
follows that the individual, as he rehearses the life of
the species, is apt to carry his taste for poetry further along than he carries his religion—that if his
development is arrested at any stage before complete

intellectual maturity that arrest is far more likely to leave him with poetical hallucinations than it is to leave him with theological hallucinations. Thus, taking men in the mass, there are many more natural victims of the former than of the latter—and here is where the talent of the ancient Jews does its execution. It holds countless thousands to the faith who are actually against the faith, and the weakness with which it holds them is their weakness for poetry, *i. e.*, for the beautiful but untrue. Put into plain, harsh words most of the articles they are asked to believe would revolt them, but put into sonorous dithyrambs the same articles fascinate and overwhelm them. It is not the logical substance of the Old Testament that continues to hold the mind of modern man, for that logical substance must often revolt him, even when he is of sub-normal intelligence; it is the sonorous strophes of the ancient bards and prophets. And it is not the epistemology, or the natural history, or the ethical scheme, or the system of jurisprudence of the New Testament that melts his heart and wets his eyes; it is simply the poetical magic of the Sermon on the Mount, the exquisite parables, and the incomparable story of the Child in the Manger.

This persistence of the weakness for poetry, no doubt, explains the great growth of ritualism in an age of skepticism. Almost every day theology gets another blow from science. So badly has it been battered during the past century, indeed, that educated men now give it little more credence than they give to sorcery, its ancient ally. But squeezing out the logical nonsense does no damage to the poetry; on the contrary, it frees, and, in a sense, dignifies the poetry. Paul's chief doctrines, clearly stated, offend the intelligence intolerably, but clothed and concealed by the gorgeous vestments of the mass they separate themselves from logic entirely and take on something of the witchery of beauty. Thus there is a constant movement of Christians, and particularly of newly-intellectual Christians, from the more literal varieties of Christian faith to the more poetical varieties. The normal Babbitt, in the United States, is born a Methodist or a Baptist, but when he begins to lay by money he and his wife tend to go over to the American branch of the Church of England, which is not only more fashionable but also less revolting to the higher cerebral centers. His daughter, when she emerges from the finishing-school, is very High Church; his grand-daughter, if the family keeps its securities, will probably go over to Rome.

In view of all this, I am convinced that the Christian church, as a going concern, is quite safe from danger, despite the rapid growth of agnosticism. The theology it merchants is full of childish and disgusting absurdities; practically all the other religions of civilized and semi-civilized man are more plausible. But all of these religions, including even Moslemism, contain the fatal defect that they appeal primarily to the reason. Christianity will survive not only Modernism but also Fundamentalism, a much more difficult business. It will survive because it makes its first and foremost appeal to that moony sense of the poetic which is in all men—to that elemental sentimentality which, in men of arrested mental development, which is to say, in the average men of Christendom, passes for the passion to seek and know beauty.

3

The Devotee

If religion is thus charming to the more enlightened modern Christian only in proportion as it is poetical, *i. e.*, as it is regarded as not literally true, it is charming to the enlightened spectator only when it is formal and hence more or less insincere. A devotee on her knees in some abysmal and mysterious cathedral, the while solemn music sounds, and clouds of incense come down the wind, and priests in luxurious, levantine costumes busy themselves with stately ceremonials in a dead and not too respectable language—this is unquestionably beautiful, particularly if the devotee herself be sightly. But the same devotee aroused to hysterical protestations of faith by the shrieks and contortions of a Methodist dervish in the costume of a Southern member of Congress, her knees trembling with the fear of God, her hands clenched as if to do combat with Beelzebub, her lips discharging hosannas and hallelujahs—this is merely obscene.

4

The Restoration of Beauty

I have said that the poetry which safeguards Christianity from destruction today was borrowed from the ancient Jews, authors of the two Testaments. But there was a long period during which it was overshadowed by purely logical ideas, many of them of a sort that would be called bolshevistic today. The principal Christians of the apostolic age were almost exactly like the modern Calvinists and Wesleyans—men quite without taste or imagination, whoopers and shouters, low vulgarians, cads. So far as is known, their public worship was wholly devoid of the sense of beauty; their sole concern was with the salvation of their so-called souls. Thus they left us nothing worth preserving—not a single church, or liturgy, or even hymn. The objects of art exhumed from the Catacombs are inferior to the drawings and statuettes of Crô-Magnon man. All the moving beauty that adorns the corpse of Christianity today came into being long after the Fathers had perished. The faith was centuries old before Christians began to build cathedrals, and nearly a thousand years old before they learned how to build good ones. It was twelve hundred years old before they invented mariolatry—the prime cause of the appearance of a purely Christian poetry. We think of Christmas as the typical Christian festival, and no doubt it is; none other is so generally kept by Christian sects, or so rich in charm and beauty. Well, Christmas, as we now have it, was almost unknown in Christendom until the Eleventh Century, when the relics of St. Nicholas of Myra, originally the patron of pawnbrokers, were brought from the East to Italy. At this time the Universal Church was already torn by controversies and menaced by schisms, and the shadow of the Reformation was plainly discernible in the West. Religions, in fact, like castles, sunsets and women, never reach their maximum of beauty until they are touched by decay.

5

End-Product

Christendom may be defined briefly as that part of the world in which, if any man stands up in public

and solemnly swears that he is a Christian, all his
auditors will laugh.

6

Another

At the end of one millennium and nine centuries
of Christianity, it remains an unshakable assumption
of the law in all Christian countries and of the moral
judgment of Christians everywhere that if a man and
a woman, entering a room together, close the door
behind them, the man will come out sadder and the
woman wiser.

7

Holy Clerks

Around no class of men do more false assumptions
cluster than around the rev. clergy, our lawful com-
missioners at the Throne of Grace. I proceed at
once to a crass example: the assumption that clergymen are necessarily religious. Obviously, it is
widely cherished, even by clergymen themselves.
The most ribald of us, in the presence of a holy clerk,
is a bit self-conscious, reticent and awed. I am
myself given to criticizing Divine Providence some-

what freely, but in the company of the rector of my
parish, even at the *Biertisch*, I tone down my ani-
madversions to a level of feeble and polite remon-
strance. I know the fellow too well, of course, to
have any actual belief in his piety. He is, in fact,
rather less pious than the average right-thinking
Americano, and I doubt gravely that the sorceries he
engages in professionally every day awaken in him
any emotion more lofty than boredom. I have heard
him pray for Coolidge, for the heathen and for rain,
but I have never heard him pray for himself. Nevertheless, the public assumption that he is highly devout, though I dispute it, colors all my intercourse
with him, and deprives him of hearing some of my
most searching and intelligent observations.

All that is needed to expose the hollowness of this
ancient delusion is to consider the chain of causes
which brings a young man to taking holy orders. Is
it, in point of fact, an irresistible religious impulse
that sets him to studying exegetics, homiletics and
the dog-Greek of the New Testament, and an irresistible religious impulse only, or is it something quite
different? I believe that it is something quite different, and that that something may be described briefly
as a desire to shine in the world without too much
effort. The young theologue, in brief, is commonly
an ambitious but somewhat lazy and incompetent
fellow, and he studies theology instead of medicine

or law because it offers a quicker and easier route to an assured job and public respect. The sacred sciences may be nonsensical bores, but they at least have the vast virtue of short-circuiting, so to speak, the climb up the ladder of security. The young doctor, for a number of years after he graduates, either has to work for nothing or to content himself with the dregs of practise, and the young lawyer, unless he has unusual influence or complete atrophy of the conscience, often teeters on the edge of actual starvation. But the young divine is a safe and distinguished man the moment he is ordained; indeed, his popularity, especially among the faithful who are fair, is often greater at that moment than it ever is afterward. His livelihood is assured instantly. At one stroke, he becomes a person of dignity and importance, eminent in his community, deferred to even by those who question his magic, and vaguely and pleasantly feared by those who credit it.

These facts, you may be sure, are not concealed from ambitious young men of the sort I have mentioned. Such young men have eyes, and even a certain capacity for ratiocination. They observe the nine sons of the police sergeant: one a priest at twenty-five, with a fine house to live in, invitations to all christenings and birthday parties for miles around, and plenty of time to go to the ball-game on Summer afternoons; the others struggling desperately to make their livings as piano-movers, tin-roofers, motormen or bootleggers. They observe the young Methodist dominie in his Ford sedan, flitting about among the women while their husbands labor down in the yards district, a clean collar around his neck, a solid meal of fried chicken in his gizzard, and his name in the local paper every day. They observe the Baptist dervish in his white necktie, raiding saloons, touring the bawdy-houses and raising hell generally, his tabernacle packed every Sunday night, a noble clink of silver in his collection-plates, and a fat purse for him now and then from the Ladies' Aid or the Ku Klux Klan. Only crazy women ever fall in love with young doctors or lawyers, but every young clergyman, if he is so inclined, may have a whole harem, and with infinitely less danger than a struggling lawyer, a bootlegger or a bank clerk runs every day. Even if he is celibate, the gals bathe him in their smiles; in truth, the more celibate he is, the more attention he gets from them. No wonder his high privileges and immunities propagate the sin of envy! No wonder there are still candidates for the holy shroud, despite the vast growth of atheism among us!

It seems to me that the majority of the young men who are thus sucked into holy orders are not actually pious at all, but rather somewhat excessively realistic —that genuine piety is far more apt to keep a youth

out of the pulpit than to take him into it. The true
devotee, frequenting the sacred edifice constantly,
becomes too familiar with the daily duties of a
clergyman to see any religious satisfaction in them.
In the main, they have nothing to do with religion
at all, but are basically social or commercial. In
so far as a clergyman works at all, he works as the
general manager of a corporation, and only too often
it is in financial difficulties and rent by factions
among the stockholders. His specifically religious
duties are of a routine and monotonous nature, and
must needs depress him mightily, as a surgeon is
depressed by the endless snaring of tonsils and ex-
cision of appendices. He debases spiritual exalta-
tion by reducing it to a hollow and meaningless
formality, as a politician debases patriotism and a
lady of joy debases love. He becomes, in the end,
quite anæsthetic to religion, and even hostile to it.
The fact is made distressingly visible by the right
rev. the bench of bishops. For a bishop to fall on
his knees spontaneously and begin to pray to God
would make almost as great a scandal as if he
mounted his throne in a bathing-suit. The piety of
the ecclesiastic, on such high levels, becomes wholly
formal and theoretical. The servant of God has
been lifted so near to the saints and become so
familiar with the inner workings of the divine machinery that the sense of awe and wonder has oozed

out of him. He can no more undergo a genuine religious experience than a veteran scene-shifter can laugh at the wheezes of the First Gravedigger. It is, perhaps, well that this is so. If the higher clergy were actually religious some of their own sermons and pastoral epistles would scare them to death.

IV. JUSTICE UNDER DEMOCRACY

1

PERHAPS the chief victims of Prohibition in the Republic, in the long run, will turn out to be the Federal judges. I do not argue here, of course, that drinking bootleg liquors will kill them bodily; I merely suggest that enforcing the unjust and insane provisions of the Volstead Act will rob them of all their old dignity. A dozen years ago a Federal judge was perhaps the most dignified and respected official yet flourishing under our democracy. The plain people, many years before that, had lost all respect for lawmakers, whether Federal, State or municipal, and save for the President himself, they had very little respect left for the gentlemen of the executive arm, high or low. More, they had begun to view the judiciary of the States very biliously, and showed no sign of surprise when a member of it was taken in judicial adultery. But for the Federal judges they still continued to have a high veneration, and for plain reasons. *Imprimis,* the Federal judges sat for life, and thus did not have to climb down from their benches at intervals and clamor obscenely for votes. Secondly, the laws that they were told off to enforce, and especially the criminal laws, were few in number, simple in character, and thoroughly in accord with almost universal ideas of right and wrong. No citizen in his right mind had much sympathy for the felons who were shipped to Atlanta each morning by the marshals of the Federal courts—chiefly counterfeiters, fraudulent bankrupts, adulterators of food and drugs, get-rich-quick swindlers, thieving letter-carriers, crooked army officers, and so on. Public sentiment was almost unanimously behind the punishment of such rogues, and it rejoiced that that punishment was in the hands of men who carried on the business in an austere and elevated manner, without fear and without favor. It was, in those days, almost unheard of for a petit jury in a Federal court to acquit a prisoner whose guilt was plain; the percentage of convictions in some jurisdictions ran beyond ninety per cent. For guilt of the kind then dealt with by those courts met with the reprehension of practically all men not professional criminals themselves—and Federal juries, petit and grand, were picked with some care, as Federal judges themselves were picked.

I describe a Golden Age, now lamentably closed. The Uplift in its various lovely forms has completely changed the character of the work done by a Fed-

eral judge.   Once the dispenser of varieties of law
that only scoundrels questioned, he is now the harassed and ludicrous dispenser of varieties of law
that only idiots approve.   It was the Espionage Act,
I suppose, that brought him to this new and dreadful
office, but it is Prohibition—whether of wine-bibbing,
of drug-taking, of interstate week-ending, or of what
not—that has carried him beyond the bounds of
what, to most normal men, is common decency.   His
typical job today, as a majority of the plain people
see it, especially in the big cities, is simply to punish
men who have refused or been unable to pay the
bribes demanded by Prohibition enforcement officers.   In other words, he is now chiefly appre-
hended by the public, not as a scourge of rascals, but
as an agent of rascals and a scourge of peaceable
men.   He gets a great deal more publicity than he
used to get in his palmy days, but it is publicity of
a sort that rapidly undermines his dignity.   Unfortunately for him, but perhaps very fortunately for
what remains of civilized government among us, the
plain people have never been able to grasp the difference between law and justice.   To them the two
things are one—or ought to be.   So the fact that the
judge is bound by law to enforce all the intolerable
provisions of the Volstead Act, including even its
implicit provision that men wearing its badges shall
get a fair percentage upon every transaction in boot-

legging—this fact does not relieve the judge himself of responsibility for the ensuing injustice. All that the vulgar observe is that justice has departed from his courtroom. Once the equal of an archbishop, he is now the equal of a police captain; once respected, he is now distrusted and disliked.

If this were all, of course, it might be possible to dismiss the whole matter on the ground that the public is an ass. That men of the highest worth are not always respected, even when they wear official robes, is a commonplace. But in the present case there is more to it than merely that. Not a few of the Federal judges have begun to show signs that the noisome work that has been forced upon them has begun to achieve its inevitable subjective effects; in other words, not a few begin to attack their sneaking sense of its lack of dignity and good repute by bedizening it with moral indignation. The judicial servant of the Anti-Saloon League thus takes on some of the neo-Christian character of the League's own dervishes and sorcerers. He is not content to send some poor yokel to jail for an artificial crime that, in the view of at least eighty per cent. of all even half-civilized Americans, is no crime at all; he must also denounce the culprit from the bench in terms fit for a man accused of arson or mayhem. Here the Freudians, perhaps, may have something to say; the great masses of the innocent and sinful, knowing nothing of Freud, observe only that the learned jurist is silly as well as unjust. There issues from that observation a generally bilious view of his office and his person. He slides slowly down a fatal chute. His day of arctic and envied eminence passes. A few sensitive judges quietly retire from the bench. But the legal mind is usually tougher than that. It can almost always find justification for doing, as agent of the law, what would be inconceivable privately to a man of honor.

2

The truth is, indeed, that the decline in dignity from which the Federal judges now suffer is not wholly due to the external fact of Prohibition; it is due quite as much to their own growing pliancy and lack of professional self-respect. All that Prohibition does to them is to make brilliantly plain, even to the meanest understanding, their lamentable departure from that high integrity of purpose, that assiduous concern for justice, that jealous watchfulness over the rights of man which simple men, at all times and everywhere, like to find in the judges set over them, and which the simple men of the United States, not so long ago, saw or thought they saw in the learned ornaments of the Federal bench. Before ever Volstead emerged from the Christian

Endeavor belt with his preposterous Act, confidence had begun to shake. The country had seen Federal judges who were unmistakably mountebanks; it had seen some who were, to the naked eye, indistinguishable from rascals. It had seen one step down from the highest court in the land to engage in an undignified stumping-tour, soliciting the votes of the rabble. It had seen another diligently insinuate himself into the headlines of the yellow press, in competition with Jack Dempsey and Babe Ruth. It had seen others abuse their powers of equity in the frank interest of capital, and deny the commonest justice to poor men in their clutches. And during the war it had grown accustomed to seeing the Federal bench converted into a sort of rival to the rostrum of Liberty Loan orators, with judges hurling pious objurgations at citizens accused of nothing worse than speaking their minds freely, and all pretense to fair hearings and just punishments abandoned.

Of late the multiplication of such Dogberries has gone on apace as the best of the old-time judges have retired from the bench. These new jurisconsults, rejecting justice openly and altogether, have even begun to reject the Constitution and the law. A judicial process before them is indistinguishable from a bull-fight, with the accused, if he is unpopular enough, as the bull. It is their theory, apparently, that the sole function of a judge is to fill the jails.

If the accused happens to be guilty or to be reasonably suspected of guilt, well and good. But if, as in the Chicago Socialist trials, he is obviously innocent, to hell with him anyhow. True enough, a majority of the Federal judges, high and low, still stand clear of such buffooneries. Even in the midst of the worst hysteria of the war there were plenty who refused to be run amok by Palmer, Burleson and company; I need cite only Hand, J., and Rose, J., as admirable examples of a number of judges who preserved their dignity 'mid the rockets' red glare. But the headlines in the newspapers had nothing to say about such judges; their blackest ink was reserved for the other kind. That other kind gradually established a view of the Federal bench that still persists, and that is growing more and more fixed as the farce of Prohibition enforcement unrolls. It is a view which, in brief, holds that the Federal bench is no longer the most exalted and faithful protector of the liberties of the citizen, but the most relentless and inordinate foe of them—that its main purpose is not to dispense justice at all, but to get men into jail, guilty or not guilty, by fair means or foul— that to this end it is willing to lend itself to the execution of any law, however extravagant, and to support that execution with a variety of casuistry that is flatly against every ordinary conception of common sense and common decency. The Espionage Act cases, the la-

bor injunction cases, the deportation cases, the Postal
Act cases, the Mann Act cases, and now the Prohibition cases—all of these, impinging in rapid succession
upon a people brought up to regard the Bill of Rights
as a reality and liberty as a precious thing, have
bred suspicion of the Federal courts, including especially the Supreme Court, and, on the heels of that
suspicion, a positive and apparently ineradicable distrust.   I doubt that the Radical fanatics who dodge
about the land have ever converted any substantial
body of Americans to their crazy doctrines; certainly
there is not the slightest sign today of the Revolution that they were predicting for last year, and the
year before.   But when they have denounced the
Federal courts and produced the overwhelming evidence, their shots have gone home.

Now and then a judge has argued, defending himself against some manifestation of popular discontent, that he is helpless—that he is the agent, not of
justice, but of law.   Even in the hey-day of the Espionage Act a few were moved to make that apology
from the bench, including, if I remember rightly,
the judge who sentenced Debs.   The distinction thus
set up is one that seems clear to lawyers, but, as I
have said, it seldom gets a hospitable hearing from
plain men.   If the latter believe anything at all it
is that law without justice is an evil thing—that such
law, indeed, leads inevitably to a contradiction in

terms—that the highest duty of the judiciary is not
to enforce it pedantically, but to evade it, vitiate it,
and, if possible, destroy it. The plain man sees
plenty of other sorts of law destroyed by the courts;
he can't help wondering why the process is so seldom
applied to statutes that violate, not merely legal
apothegms, but the baldest of common sense. Thus
when he beholds a Federal judge fining a man, under
a constitutional amendment prohibiting the sale of
intoxicating beverages, for selling a beverage that
is admittedly not intoxicating, or jailing another man
who has got before the bar, as everyone knows, not
because he ran a still but because he refused to
pay the bribe demanded by the Prohibition enforcement officer, or issuing against a third an injunction whose sole and undisguised purpose is to deprive
him, by a legal swindle, of his constitutional right
to a trial by jury of his peers—when he observes such
monkey-shines going on in the name of the law, is
it any wonder that he concludes dismally that the
law is an ass, and its agent another? In ordinary
life men cannot engage in such lunatic oppressions
of their fellow-men without paying a penalty for
it; even a policeman must be measurably more plausible and discreet. If a judge is bound by his oath
to engage in them, then so much the worse for the
judge. He can no more hope to be respected than
a hangman can hope to be respected.

The truth is, of course, that the judges are by no means under the compulsion that is alleged. The injunction clause of the Volstead Act actually has no constitutional mandate behind it; the only constitutional mandate that I can find, bearing upon it at all, is against it. That is to be found in the Fifth and Sixth Amendments. The first of these amendments provides that "no person shall be held to answer for a capital or otherwise infamous crime unless on a presentment or indictment of a grand jury"; the second requires that "in all criminal prosecutions the accused shall enjoy the right to a speedy and public trial by an impartial jury of the State and district wherein the crime shall have been committed." It must be obvious to everyone that the aim of the injunction clause is simply and solely to deprive the accused of these safeguards—to rob him of his clear right to a trial by a jury of his peers. The history of the clause reveals the fact clearly. It was first heard of in Iowa in the early years of the century, and it was invented there, not by Prohibitionists, but by the frantic vice-crusaders who then raged and roared in the hinterland, inflaming the pious with gaudy yarns about white slave traders, seducers armed with hypodermic syringes, and other such phantasms. In Iowa these vice-crusaders specialized in the harassing of the sort of poor women who keep cheap lodging-houses. When such a woman, by ignorance or inadvertance, admitted a lady no longer a lady to her establishment, they raided her, dragged her to jail, and charged her with keeping a bawdy-house. This was good sport, and the rev. pastors urged it on every Sunday. But after the first uproar, it began to develop defects, and the chief of these defects was that juries refused to convict. Now and then a man of sense and self-respect got upon the panel and spoiled the show. Perhaps he found it impossible to believe the sworn testimony of the vice-crusaders. Perhaps he concluded that the accused, though guilty, had been punished enough by the raid. Whatever his motive, he hung the jury and killed the hunting.

It was then that Christian lawyers came to the rescue of pious and baffled men. They did it by the simple process of throwing the whole responsibility upon the judge. Juries were hard to intimidate; there was always apt to be at least one juror who didn't care a hoot what was said against him from the sacred desk—some hell-cat who positively rejoiced in the indignation of the knock-'em-down-and-drag-'em-out clergy. But judges were tenderer. Some of them were candidates for re-election to the bench; all of them were solicitous about their dignity, and did not care to face ecclesiastical curses, pious whispers, suggestive winks. So the Iowa lawyers amended the law by inventing and inserting the injunction clause.   This clause flatly abolished the right of trial by jury.   When the vice-crusaders found a likely victim they simply got a friendly judge to issue an injunction against her, restraining her from using her premises for immoral purposes.   Then they watched her closely.   The moment they detected a dubious female entering her door they raided her again, dragged her before the same judge—and he jailed her for contempt of court, an offense punishable summarily and without a jury trial.   Nine times out of ten, perhaps, a jury would have acquitted her, but the judge was already safely against her.

This scheme gave the vice-crusaders a new lease of life and greatly increased their takings in the Sunday-schools.   Naturally enough, the Prohibitionists, who were, in most cases, none other than the vice-crusaders themselves, instantly borrowed it, and so it got into the Prohibition acts of all the dry States.   Volstead, as a country State's attorney on the Minnesota steppes, employed it diligently and to vast effect.   He put it into the Volstead Act as a matter of course.   There it stands today, a dishonest and disgraceful blemish upon American law.   Its deliberate aim is to take away from the citizen accused of crime his constitutional right to a jury trial; no imaginable argument in favor of it can dodge that plain fact.   When it is invoked, as under the Volstead Act, against a man who has been found guilty of one violation of the act, it not only punishes him doubly for that violation; it also punishes him in advance for a second offense that he has admittedly not committed, and deprives him of his constitutional means of defense in case he is subsequently accused. He is, in brief, put absolutely at the mercy of the judge—and the judge is already obviously suspicious of him, and may be a senile sadist or Prohibitionist demagogue to boot. The constitutional provision that a man accused of crime may throw himself upon a jury of plain men like himself, sworn to regard only the evidence actually before them—that if he is able to convince only one of the twelve that he is innocent, or not proved guilty beyond a doubt, he shall go free—this fundamental guarantee of the citizen, this most sacred of all human rights under Anglo-Saxon jurisprudence, is specifically nullified and made a mock of in order to satisfy the frenzy of a minority of fanatics!

That contempt of court should be an offense standing outside the purview of the Fifth and Sixth Amendments—that a judge should have the power to punish summarily all deliberate floutings of his dignity— this may be reasonably argued, though there are many sound considerations against it. But that it should be lawful to convert some other and wholly unrelated offense into contempt of court by a legal fiction, and so get around the Fifth and Sixth Amend-

ments by a swindle—this is surely more than any
sensible man would soberly maintain. When it is
maintained, it is only by persons who are trying
to put men into jail by processes that any average
jury would revolt against—mill owners eager to get
rid of annoying labor leaders, coal operators bent
upon making slaves of their miners, Prohibitionists
lusting for the punishment of their opponents. The
injunction in strike cases has been a stench for
years; it is, indeed, so bad that a large number of
Federal judges refuse absolutely to employ it. It
is a worse stench in Prohibition cases, for here it is
becoming a formidable and favorite weapon, not
merely in the hands of property-owners who want
to put down strikes, but in the hands of criminal
Prohibition agents who seek to wring blackmail from
their victims. In brief, it has become a dishonest
means of oppression for men who are even more dishonest than it is. Certainly it is idle to talk of
respect for the laws when such devices have legislative and judicial sanction. No reasonable man,
save he be ignorant of their nature and purpose, can
conceivably respect them. If, on the ground that
whatever is in the law should be given full faith and
credit, he maintains that they should not be resisted,
then he maintains that the Bill of Rights is no more
than a string of empty phrases, and that any shyster

who invents a way to evade and abrogate it is a jurist
as dignified as John Marshall.

3

Is a judge bound to lend himself to such gross and
dishonest attacks upon the common rights of the citizen? I am no lawyer, but I presume to doubt it.
There were judges in 1918 who did not think themselves obliged to sacrifice the Bill of Rights to the
Espionage Act, and who resolutely refused to do so,
and yet, so far as I know, nothing happened to them;
at least one of them, to my knowledge, has been
since promoted to a circuit. Why should any judge
enforce the injunction clause of the Volstead Act?
Its enforcement is surely not an automatic act; it involves deliberation and decision by the judge; he may
refuse his injunction without offering any explanation to anyone. What would follow if he arose one
day in his high pulpit, and announced simply that his
court was purged of all such oblique and dishonest
enactments henceforth—that he had resolved to refuse to lend himself to the schemes of blackmailers
with badges, or to harass and punish free citizens in
violation of their fundamental constitutional rights
and their plain dignity as human beings, or, in brief,
to engage in any other enterprise as a judge that he

would shrink from engaging in as a good citizen and a man of honor?   Would the result be impeachment? I should like to meet a Congressman insane enough to move the impeachment of such a judge!   Would it be a storm of public indignation? . . . Or would it be a vociferous yell of delight?

It seems to me, indeed, that the first judge who rises to such a rebellion will be the first judge ever to become a popular hero in the Republic—that he will be elevated to the Supreme Court by a sort of acclamation, even if it is necessary to get rid of one of the sitting justices by setting fire to his gown.   But even imagining him so elevated, the remaining eight justices will still function, and all of us know what they think of the Bill of Rights.   Wouldn't such a rebel judge succumb to the system of which he was a discreet particle?   Couldn't the other eight judges nullify and make a mock of his heroic defiance? Could they, indeed?   Then how?   If a judge, high or low, actually called in justice to rescue a citizen from the law, what precisely could the Supreme Court do about it?   I know of no appeal by the District Attorney in criminal cases, once the accused has been put in jeopardy; I know only of impeachment for judges who forget the lines of the solemn farce to which they are sworn.   But try to imagine the impeachment of a judge charged with punching a hole in the Volstead Act, and letting in some common justice and common decency!

So far, no such rambunctious and unprecedented judge has been heard of,—none, that is, has objected to the injunction clause in toto and head on—nor do I specifically predict his advent. He may come, but probably he won't. The law is a curse to all of us, but it is a curse of special virulence to lawyers. It becomes for them a sort of discreditable vice, a stealthy and degrading superstition. It robs them of all balance, of all capacity for clear thought, of all imagination. Judges tend to show this decay of the faculties in an exaggerated form; they become mere automata, bound by arbitrary rules, precedents, the accumulated imbecilities of generations of bad logic; to their primary lack of sense as lawyers they add the bombastic manner of bureaucrats. It is thus too much to hope for a judge showing any originality or courage; one Holmes in an era of Hardings and Coolidges is probably more than a fair allotment. But while the judges of the District Courts go on driving wild teams of jackasses through the Bill of Rights, and the rev. seniors of the Supreme Court give their approval to the business in solemn form, sometimes but not always with Holmes, J., and Brandeis, J., dissenting—while all this is going on, there are black clouds rolling up from the hinterland, where the Constitution is still taught in the schools and even Methodists are bred to reverence Patrick Henry. The files of Congress already show the way the wind is blowing—constitutional amendments to drag down and denaturize the Supreme Court, simple acts to the same end, other acts providing for the election of Federal judges, yet others even more revolutionary. I know of no such proposal that has any apparent merit. Even the best of them, hamstringing the courts, would only augment the power of a Congress that is ten times worse. But so long as judges pursue fatuously the evil business of converting every citizen into a subject, demagogues will come forward with their dubious remedies, and, soon or late, unless the bench pulls up, some of these demagogues will get themselves heard.

V. REFLECTIONS ON HUMAN MONOGAMY

1

The Eternal Farce

AS every attentive patron of the drama is well aware, it is difficult for even the most skillful actors to keep Ibsen's "Hedda Gabler" from degenerating to farce in the performance. The reason is certainly not occult. It lies in the plain fact that such transactions as the dramatist here deals with—a neurotic woman's effort to be heavily romantic, her horror when romance is followed by pregnancy, the manœuvres of a satanic and idiotic lover, the cuckolding of a husband wearing whiskers —are intrinsically and incurably farcical. *All* love affairs, in truth, are farcical—that is, to the spectators. When one hears that some old friend has succumbed to the blandishments of a sweet one, however virtuous and beautiful she may be, one does not gasp and roll one's eyes; one simply laughs. When one hears, a year or two later, that they are quarreling, one laughs again. When one hears that the bride is

seeking consolation from the curate of the parish, one
laughs a third time.   When one hears that the bride-
groom, in revenge, is sneaking his stenographer to dinner at an Italian restaurant, one laughs a fourth time.
And so on.   But when one goes to the theatre, the
dramatist often asks one to wear a solemn frown when
he displays the same puerile and ludicrous phenomena
—that is, while he depicts a fat actress as going crazy
when she discovers that her husband, an actor with a
face like the abdomen of a ten-pin, has run off to
Asbury Park, N. J., with another actress who pro-
nounces all French words in the manner of the Texas
Christian University.

The best dramatists, of course, make no such mistake.   In Shakespeare love is always depicted as
comedy—sometimes light and charming, as in
"Twelfth Night," but usually rough and buffoonish,
as in "The Taming of the Shrew."   This comic attitude is plainly visible even in such plays as "Hamlet" and "Romeo and Juliet."   In its main outlines,
I suppose, "Hamlet" is properly looked upon as a
tragedy, but if you believe that the love passages are
intended to be tragic then all I ask is that you give a
sober reading to the colloquies between Hamlet and
Ophelia.   They are not only farcical; they are downright obscene; Shakespeare, through the mouth of
Hamlet, derides the whole business with almost intolerable ribaldry.   As for "Romeo and Juliet,"

what is it but a penetrating burlesque upon the love guff that was fashionable in the poet's time? True enough, his head buzzed with such loveliness that he could not write even burlesque without making it beautiful—compare "Much Ado About Nothing" and "Othello"—but nevertheless it is quite absurd to say that he was serious when he wrote this tale of calf-love. Imagine such a man taking seriously the spasms and hallucinations of a *Backfisch* of fourteen, the tinpot heroics of a boy of eighteen! Shakespeare remembered very well the nature of his own amorous fancies at eighteen. It was the year of his seduction by Ann Hathaway, whose brothers later made him marry her, much to his damage and dismay. He wrote the play at forty-five. Tell it to the Marines!

I have a suspicion that even Ibsen, though he seldom permitted himself overt humor, indulged in some quiet spoofing when he wrote "A Doll's House," "Hedda Gabler," "The Lady From the Sea" and "Little Eyolf." The whole last act of "Hedda Gabler" could be converted into burlesque by changing ten words; as I have said, it is almost always burlesque as bad actors play it. In the cases of "Ghosts" and "The Master-Builder" there can be no doubt whatever. The former is a piece of buffoonery designed to make fun of the fools who were outraged by "A Doll's House"; the latter is a comic piece founded upon personal experience. At the age of sixty Ibsen amused himself with a flirtation with a girl of sixteen. Following the custom of her sex, she took his casual winks and cheek-pinchings quite seriously, and began hinting to the whole neighborhood that the old boy was hopelessly gone on her, and that he intended to divorce Fru Ibsen and run off with her to Italy. All this gave entertainment to Ibsen, who was a sardonic man, and he began speculating as to what would happen to a man of his age who actually yielded to the gross provocations of such a wench. The result was "The Master-Builder." But think of the plot! He makes the master-builder climb a church-steeple, and then jump off! Imagine him regarding such slap-stick farce seriously!

The world has very little sense of humor. It is always wagging its ears solemnly over elaborate jocosities. For 600 years it has gurgled over the "Divine Comedy" of Dante, despite the plain fact that the work is a flaming satire upon the whole Christian hocus-pocus of heaven, purgatory and hell. To have tackled such nonsense head-on, in Dante's time, would have been to flout the hangman; hence the poet clothed his attack in an irony so delicate that the ecclesiastical police were baffled. Why is the poem called a comedy? I have read at least a dozen discussions of the question by modern pedants, all of them labored and unconvincing. The same problem obviously engaged the scholars of the poet's own time.

He called the thing simply "comedy"; they added the adjective "divine" in order to ameliorate what seemed to them to be an intolerable ribaldry. Well, here is a "comedy" in which human beings are torn limb from limb, boiled in sulphur, cut up with red-hot knives, and filled with molten lead! Can one imagine a man capable of such a poem regarding such fiendish imbecilities seriously? Certainly not. They appeared just as idiotic to him as they appear to you or me. But the Federal judiciary of the day made it impossible to say so in plain language, so he said so behind a smoke-screen of gaudy poetry. How Dante would have roared if he could have known that six hundred years later an illiterate President of the United States, a good Baptist with money in the bank, married happily to a divorcée—would take the whole thing with utter seriousness, and deliver a nonsensical harangue upon the lessons in it for American Christians!

The case of Wagner's "Parsifal" is still more remarkable. Even Nietzsche was deceived by it. Like the most maudlin German fat woman at Baireuth, he mistook the composer's elaborate and outrageous burlesque of Christianity for a tribute to Christianity, and so denounced him as a jackass and refused to speak to him thereafter. To this day "Parsifal" is given with all the trappings of a religious ceremonial, and pious folks go to hear it who would instantly shut their ears if the band began playing "Tristan und Isolde." It has become, in fact, a sort of " 'Way Down East" or "Ben Hur" of music drama—a bait for luring patrons who are never seen in the opera-house otherwise. But try to imagine such a thumping atheist as Wagner writing a religious opera seriously! And if, by any chance, you succeed in imagining it, then turn to the Char-Freitag music, and play it on your victrola. Here is the central scene of the piece, the moment of most austere solemnity—and to it Wagner fits music that is so luscious and so fleshly—indeed, so downright lascivious and indecent—that even I, who am almost anæsthetic to such provocations, blush every time I hear it. The Flower Maidens do not raise my blood-pressure a single ohm; I have actually snored through the whole second act of "Tristan." But when I hear that Char-Freitag music all of my Freudian suppressions begin groaning and stretching their legs in the dungeons of my unconscious. And what does Char-Freitag mean? Char-Freitag means Good Friday!

2

Venus at the Domestic Hearth

One inclines to the notion that women—and especially homely women—greatly overestimate the importance of physical beauty in their eternal con-spiracy against the liberty of men. It is a powerful lure, to be sure, but it is certainly not the only one that fetches the game, nor even, perhaps, the most effective one. The satisfaction that a man gets out of conquering—which is to say, out of succumbing to—a woman of noticeable pulchritude is chiefly the rather banal one of parading her before other men. He likes to show her off as he likes to show his ex-pensive automobile or his big door-knob factory. It is her apparent costliness that is her principal charm. Her beauty sets up the assumption that she was sought eagerly by other men, some of them wealthy, and that it thus took a lot of money or a lot of skill to obtain the monopoly of her.

But very few men are so idiotic that they are blind to the hollowness of such satisfactions. A husband, after all, spends relatively few hours of his life parading his wife, or even contemplating her beauty. What engages him far more often is the unromantic business of living with her—of listening to her conversation, of trying to fathom and satisfy her whims, of detecting and counteracting her plots against his ego, of facing with her the dull hazards and boredoms of everyday life. In the discharge of this business personal beauty is certainly not nec-essarily a help; on the contrary, it may be a down-right hindrance, if only because it makes for the

hollowest and least intelligent of all forms of vanity.
Of infinitely more value is a quality that women too
often neglect, to wit, the quality of simple amiability.   The most steadily charming of all human
beings, male or female, is the one who is tolerant,
unprovocative, good-humored, kind.   A man wants
a show only intermittently, but he wants peace and
comfort every day.   And to get them, if he is saga-
cious, he is quite willing to sacrifice scenery.

3

The Rat-trap

Much of the discontent with modern marriage centers in the fact that the laws which condition it and
safeguard it all assume that its purpose is the founding of a family.   This was unquestionably its purpose when those laws were devised, say three thousand years ago, but that purpose, at least among the
civilized minority, is now almost forgotten.   Very
few educated men of today, it seems to me, have any
notion of founding a family in mind when they
marry.   Their vanity takes different forms; moreover, they have rejected the old doctrine that they
have any duty in the premises; the *Stammhalter* has
pretty well disappeared from their visions.   Most
of them, it is probable, marry without any intelligible

purpose whatever. Women flatter them, mark them
down and lure them to the holy altar: everything else
is afterthought. Many an American man finds himself on the brink of marriage without ever having
given any sober thought even to so important a matter as the probable charm of his bride-elect as mistress. This explains many connubial calamities.

As things stand, the only legal relief from uncomfortable marriages is afforded by divorce.
Every other workable device is frowned upon, and
most of them are punished. The chief purpose of
legal divorce, of course, is to protect the children of
the marriage, *i. e.*, to safeguard the family. But the
scheme is clumsy, expensive and cruel. To employ
it is to cut off a leg in order to cure what may be,
after all, merely a barked shin—worse, what may
be no injury at all. Suppose there *are* no children?
Suppose the marriage is entered upon with the clear
understanding that there *shall* be no children? In
the latter case it is obviously insane to surround it
with safeguards for the family that will never exist.
As well insure a pile of bricks against fire. What
is needed is legal recognition of such marriages—
recognition that will establish decorum and fair play
within their actual limits, but that will not seek to
burden them with conditions that look quite outside
their limits. Human inertia and sentimentality, of
course, will be a long while countenancing any such

change. Until quite recently a marriage without children was utterly impossible, save as an act of God, and so the inevitable, by a familiar process, was converted into the creditable. This nonsense survives, despite the disappearance of the excuse for it. It is still believed, by the great majority of human beings, that there is something mysteriously laudable about achieving viable offspring. I have searched the sacred and profane scriptures for many years, but have yet to find any logical ground for this notion. To have a child is no more creditable than to have rheumatism—and no more discreditable. Ethically, it is absolutely meaningless. And practically, it is mainly a matter of chance.

4

The Love Chase

The notion that man is the aggressor in love is frequently supported by old-fashioned psychologists by pointing to the example of the lower animals. The lion, it appears, stalks the lioness to her shame and undoing; the amorous cock pursues the reluctant and virtuous hen. Granted. But all that this proves, giving the analogy all the value asked for it, is that man is the aggressor as *lover*, pure and simple, *i. e.*, as seducer. Is he also the aggressor as suitor and husband? To ask the question is almost to answer it. . . . Well, it is precisely his rôle of husband that differentiates man from lion and cock. And once he is thus differentiated, all his previous likeness disappears. . . . In civilized societies, there is a double stalking: for mistresses and for husbands. The fact that the majority of women retain their virtue to the altar and that the majority of men, soon or late, are married—this offers a capital indication of the relative enthusiasm and pertinacity with which the two varieties of aggression are carried on.

5

Women as Realpolitiker

Women in general are far too intelligent to have any respect for so-called ideas. One seldom hears of them suffering and dying for any of the bogus Great Truths that men believe in. When a woman is on good terms with her husband she is quite willing to accept his idiotic theorizings on any subject that happens to engage him, whether theological, economic, epistemological or political. When one hears of a Republican man who has a Democratic wife, or *vice versa*, it is always safe to assume that she has her eye on a handsomer, richer or more docile fellow, and is thinking of calling up a lawyer.

6

Footnote for Suffragettes

The double standard of morality will survive in this world so long as a woman whose husband has been debauched is favored with the sympathetic tears of other women, and a man whose wife has run away with an actor is laughed at by other men.

7

The Helpmate

The notion that a true and loving (and, let us hope, amiable and beautiful) wife inspires a man to high endeavor is largely illusory. Every sane woman knows instinctively, as a matter of fact, that the highest aspirations of her husband are fundamentally inimical to her, and that their realization is apt to cost her her possession of him. What she dreams of is not an infinitely brilliant husband, but an infinitely "solid" one, which is to say, one bound irretrievably by the chains of normalcy. It would delight her to see him get to the White House, for a man in the White House is as relentlessly policed as an archbishop. But it would give her a great deal of disquiet to see him develop into a Goethe or a Wagner.

I have known in my time a good many men of the first talent, as talent is reckoned in America, and most of them have been married. I can't recall one whose wife appeared to view his achievements with perfect ease of mind. In every case the lady was full of a palpable fear—the product of feminine intuition, *i. e.*, of hard realism and common sense—that his rise shook her hold upon him, that he became a worse husband in proportion as he became a better man. In the logic I can discern no flaw. The ideal husband is surely not a man of active and daring mind; he is the man of placid and conforming mind. Here the good business man obviously beats the artist and adventurer. His rewards are all easily translated into domestic comfort and happiness. He is not wobbled by the admiration of other women, none of whom, however much they may esteem his virtues as a husband, are under any illusion as to his virtues as a lover. Above all, his mind is not analytical, and hence he is not likely to attempt any anatomizing of his marriage—the starting point for the worst sort of domestic infelicity. No man, examining his marriage intelligently, can fail to observe that it is compounded, at least in part, of slavery, and that he is the slave. Happy the woman whose husband is so stupid that he never launches into that coroner's inquest!

8

The Mime

The fundamental objection to actors, stripping the business of all mere sophistry and snobbery, is that they give away the idiotic vanity of the whole male sex. An actor is simply a man who, by word and strut, says aloud of *him*self what all normal men think of *them*selves. Thus he exposes, in a highly indiscreet and disconcerting manner, the full force of masculine vanity. But I doubt that he exaggerates it. No healthy male is ever actually modest. No healthy male ever really thinks or talks of anything save himself. His conversation is one endless boast—often covert, but always undiluted. His politics is a mere sneering at what he conceives to be inferiors; his philosophy is simply an exposure of asses; he cannot imagine himself save as superior, dominating, the center of situations. Even his theology is seldom more than a stealthy comparison of himself and God, to the disadvantage of God. . . . The youngest flapper knows all this. Feminine strategy, in the duel of sex, consists almost wholly of an adroit feeding of this vanity. Man makes love by braggadocio. Woman makes love by listening. . . . Once a woman passes a certain point in intelligence she finds it almost impossible to get a husband: she simply cannot go on listening without snickering.

9

Cavia Cobaya

I find the following in Theodore Dreiser's "Hey-Rub-a-Dub-Dub";

Does the average strong, successful man confine himself to one woman? Has he ever?

The first question sets an insoluble problem. How are we, in such intimate matters, to say what is the average and what is not the average? But the second question is easily answered, and the answer is, He has. Here Dreiser's curious sexual obsession simply leads him into absurdity. His view of the traffic of the sexes remains the naïve one of an ex-Baptist nymph in Greenwich Village. Does he argue that Otto von Bismarck was not a "strong, successful man"? If not, then let him remember that Bismarck was a strict monogamist—a man full of sin, but always faithful to his Johanna. Again, there was Thomas Henry Huxley. Again, there was William Ewart Gladstone. Again, there was Robert Edward Lee. Yet again, there were Robert Schumann, Felix Mendelssohn, Johann Sebastian Bach,

Ulysses S. Grant, Andrew Jackson, Louis Pasteur, Martin Luther, Helmuth von Moltke, Stonewall Jackson, Lyof Tolstoi, Robert Browning, Henrik Ibsen, William T. Sherman, Carl Schurz, old Sam Adams, . . . I could extend the list to pages. . . . Perhaps I am unfair to Dreiser. His notion of a "strong, successful man" may be, not such a genuinely superior fellow as Bismarck or Bach, but such a mere brigand as Shonts, Yerkes or Jim Fisk. If so, he is still wrong. If so, he still runs aground on John D. Rockefeller.

10

The Survivor

Around every bachelor of more than thirty-five legends tend to congregate, chiefly about the causes of his celibacy. If it is not whispered that he is damaged goods, and hence debarred from marriage by a lofty concept of Service to the unborn, it is told under the breath that he was insanely in love at the age of twenty-six with a beautiful creature who jilted him for an insurance underwriter and so broke his heart beyond repair. Such tales are nearly always moonshine. The reason why the average bachelor of thirty-five remains a bachelor is really very simple. It is, in brief, that no ordinarily attractive and

intelligent woman has ever made a serious and un-
divided effort to marry him.

11

The Veteran's Disaster

The tragedy of experience is that a man no longer
believes it when a woman shows all the orthodox
signs of having been flustered by him.   In youth it
gives him immense delight to discover that he has
made a mash, but when he gets into the middle years
the thing merely annoys him.   He is irritated that
yet another female Cagliostro should try to floor him
with the immemorial mumbo-jumbo, and so make a
fool of him.   The girl he succumbs to is the one who
tells him frankly that her heart is buried in France,
but that she admires him tremendously and would
esteem it a singular honor to be the wife of so meritorious a fellow.   This helps to explain, perhaps, why
aging men so often succumb to flappers.

12

Moral Indignation

The ill-fame of the Turks in the English-speaking
world is not due to their political medievalism, as is

usually alleged, but to their practise of polygamy.
That practise inevitably excites the erotic imagination
of men doomed to monogamy, and particularly of
men doomed to monogamy with despotic, prudish and
unappetizing wives, which is to say, the normal,
typical men of England and the United States.   They
envy the Turk his larger and more charming joys,
and hence hate him.   Every time Reuter reports
him dragging a fresh herd of dark-eyed, voluptuous Georgian or Armenian women into his seraglio,
they hate him the more.   The way to arouse a Puritan to his highest pitch of moral indignation is
not to burn down an orphan-asylum; the way to do
it is to grab a pretty girl around the waist and
launch with her into the lascivious measures of a
Wiener Walz.   Men always hate most what they envy
most.

13

The Man and His Shadow

Every man, whatever his actual qualities, is
credited with and judged by certain general qualities
that are supposed to appertain to his sex, particularly
by women.   Thus man the individual is related to
Man the species, often to his damage and dismay.

Consider my own case. I am by nature one of the most orderly of mortals. I have a place for every article of my personal property, whether a Bible or a cocktail-shaker, an undershirt or an eye-dropper, and I always keep it where it belongs. I never drop cigar-ashes on the floor. I never upset a waste-basket. I am never late for trains. I never run short of collars. I never go out with a purple neck-tie on a blue shirt. I never fail to appear in time for dinner without telephoning or telegraphing. Yet the women who are cursed by God with the care of me maintain and cherish the fiction that I am an extremely careless and even hoggish fellow—that I have to be elaborately nursed, supervised and policed—that the slightest relaxation of vigilance over my everyday conduct would reduce me to a state of helplessness and chaos, with all my clothes mislaid, half my books in the ash-can, my mail unanswered, my face unshaven, and my office not unlike an I. W. W. headquarters after a raid by the *Polizei*. It is their firm theory that, unaided by superior suggestion, I'd wear one shirt six weeks, and a straw hat until Christmas. They never speak of my work-room save in terms of horror, though it is actually the most orderly room in my house. Weekly I am accused of having lost all my socks and handker-chiefs, though they are in my clothes-press all the

while.   At least once a month formal plans are discussed for reorganizing my whole mode of life, that
I may not sink into irremediable carelessness, in-
efficiency and barbarism.

I note that many other men lie under the same
benign espionage and misrepresentation—in fact,
nearly all men.   But it is my firm belief that very
few men are really disorderly.   The business of the
world is managed by getting order into it, and the
feeling for discipline thus engendered is carried over
into domestic life.   I know of very few men who
ever drop ashes on the dining-room rug, or store
their collars in their cigar-box, or put on brown socks
with their dress-clothes, or forget to turn off the water
after they have bathed, or neglect to keep dinner
engagements—and most of these few, I am firmly
convinced, do it because their women-folk expect it
of them, because it would cause astonishment and dismay if they refrained.   I myself, more than once,
have deliberately hung my hat on an electrolier, or
clomped over the parquetry with muddy shoes, or
gone out in a snowstorm without an overcoat, or come
down to dinner in a ragged collar, or filled my shirt-
box with old copies of the *Congressional Record*, or
upset a bottle of green ink, or used Old Dutch
Cleanser for shaving, or put olives into Jack Rose
cocktails, or gone without a hair-cut for three or four

weeks, or dropped an expensive beer *Seidel* upon the hard concrete of my cellar floor in order to give a certain necessary color to the superstition of my oafishness. If I failed to do such things now and then I'd become unpopular, and very justly so, for nothing is more obnoxious than a human being who is always challenging and correcting the prevailing view of him. Even now I make no protest; I merely record the facts. On my death-bed, I daresay, I shall carry on the masquerade. That is to say, I shall swallow a clinical themometer or two, upset my clam-broth over my counterpane, keep an ouija board and a set of dice under my pillow, and maybe, at the end, fall clumsily out of bed.

14

The Balance-Sheet

Marriage, as everyone knows, is chiefly an economic matter. But too often it is assumed that economics concerns only the wife's hats; it also concerns, and perhaps more importantly, the husband's cigars. No man is genuinely happy, married, who has to drink worse gin than he used to drink when he was single.

15

Yearning

Ah, that the eugenists would breed a woman as capable of laughter as the girl of twenty and as adept at knowing when not to laugh as the woman of thirty-five!

VI. THE POLITICIAN

HALF the sorrows of the world, I suppose, are caused by making false assumptions. If the truth were only easier to ascertain the remedy for them would consist simply of ascertaining it and accepting it. This business, alas, is usually impossible, but fortunately not always: now and then, by some occult process, half rational and half instinctive, the truth gets itself found out and an ancient false assumption goes overboard. I point, in the field of the social relations, to one which afflicted the human race for millenniums: that one, to wit, which credited the rev. clergy with a mysterious wisdom and awful powers. Obviously, it has ceased to trouble all the superior varieties of men. It may survive in those remote marches where human beings go to bed with the cows, but certainly it has vanished from the cities. Asphalt and the apostolic succession, indeed, seem to be irreconcilable enemies. I can think of no clergyman in any great American city today whose public dignity and influence are much above those of an ordinary Class I Babbitt. It is hard for even the most diligent and passionate of the ancient order to get upon the first pages of the newspapers; he must make a clown-show, discreditable to his fraying cloth, or he must blush unseen. When bishops begin launching thunderbolts against heretics, the towns do not tremble; they laugh. When elders denounce sin, sin only grows more popular. Imagine a city man getting a notice from the ordinary of his diocese that he had been excommunicated. It would trouble him far less, I venture, than his morning *Katzenjammer*.

The reason for all this is not hard to find. All the superior varieties of men—and even the lowest varieties of city workmen are at least superior to peasants—have simply rid themselves of their old belief in devils. Hell no longer affrights and palsies them, and so the magic of those who profess to save them from it no longer impresses them. That profession, I believe, was bogus, and its acceptance was therefore a false assumption. Being so, it made men unhappy; getting rid of it has delivered them. They are no longer susceptible to ecclesiastical alarms and extortions; *ergo*, they sleep and eat better. Think of what life must have been under such princes of damnation as Cotton Mather and Jonathan Edwards, with even bartenders and metaphysicians believing in them! And then compare it to life under Bishop Manning and the Rev. Dr. John Roach Straton, with only a few half-wits believing in them! Or turn to the backwoods of the Republic, where the devil is still feared, and with him his professional exterminators. In the country towns the clergy are still almost as influential as they were in Mather's day, and there, as everyone knows, they remain public nuisances, and civilized life is almost impossible. In such Neolithic regions nothing can go on without their consent, on penalty of anathema and hell-fire; as a result, nothing goes on that is worth recording. It is this survival of sacerdotal authority, I begin to believe, and not hookworm, malaria or the event of April 9, 1865, that is chiefly responsible for the cultural paralysis of the late Confederate States. The South lacks big cities; it is run by its country towns—and in every country town there is some Baptist *mullah* who rules by scaring the peasantry. The false assumption that his pretensions are sound, that he can actually bind and loose, that contumacy to him is a variety of cursing God—this false assumption is what makes the yokels so uneasy, so nervous, and hence so unhappy. If they could throw it off they would burn fewer Aframericans and sing more songs. If they could be purged of it they would be purged of Ku Kluxry too.

The cities got rid of that false assumption half a century ago, and have been making cultural progress ever since. Somewhat later they got rid of its brother, to wit, respect for government, and, in particular, respect for its visible agents, the police. That respect—traditional, and hence irrational—had been, for years, in increasingly unpleasant collision with a great body of obvious facts. The police, by assumption austere and almost sacrosanct, were gradually discovered to be, in reality, a pack of rogues and but little removed, save by superior impudence and enterprise, from the cut-throats and purse-snatchers they were set to catch. When, a few decades ago, the American people, at least in the big cities, began to accept them frankly for what they were—when the old false assumption of their integrity and public usefulness was quietly abandoned and a new and more accurate assumption of their roguery was adopted in its place—when this change was effected there was a measurable increase, I believe, in the public happiness. It no longer astonished anyone when policemen were taken in evildoing; indignation therefore abated, and with it its pains. If, before that time, the corps of Prohibition enforcement officers—*i. e.*, a corps of undisguised scoundrels with badges—had been launched upon the populace, there would have been a great roar of wrath, and much anguished gnashing of teeth. People would have felt themselves put upon, injured, insulted. But with the old false assumption about policemen removed from their minds, they met the new onslaught calmly and even smilingly. Today no one is indignant over the fact that the extortions of these new *Polizei* increase the cost of potable alcohol. The false assumption that the police are altruistic agents of a benevolent state has been replaced by the sound assumption that they are gentlemen engaged assiduously, like the rest of us, in finding meat and raiment for their families and in laying up funds to buy Liberty Bonds in the next war to end war. This is human progress, for it increases human happiness.

So much for the evidence. The deduction I propose to make from it is simply this: that a like increase would follow if the American people could only rid themselves of another and worse false assumption that still rides them—one that corrupts all their thinking about the great business of politics, and vastly augments their discontent and unhappiness—the assumption, that is, that politicians are divided into two classes, and that one of those classes is made up of good ones. I need not argue, I hope, that this assumption is almost universally held among us. Our whole politics, indeed, is based upon it, and has been based upon it since the earliest days. What is any political campaign save a concerted effort to turn out a set of politicians who are admittedly bad and put in a set who are thought to be better? The former assumption, I believe, is always sound; the latter is just as certainly false. For if experience teaches us anything at all it teaches us this: that a good politician, under democracy, is quite as unthinkable as an honest burglar. His very existence, indeed, is a standing subversion of the public good in every rational sense. He is not one who serves the common weal; he is simply one who preys upon the commonwealth. It is to the interest of all the rest of us to hold down his powers to an irreducible minimum, and to reduce his compensation to nothing; it is to his interest to augment his powers at all hazards, and to make his compensation all the traffic will bear. To argue that these aims are identical is to argue palpable nonsense. The politician, at his ideal best, never even remotely approximated in practise, is a necessary evil; at his worst he is an almost intolerable nuisance.

What I contend is simply that he would be measurably less a nuisance if we got rid of our old false assumption about him, and regarded him in the cold light of fact. At once, I believe, two-thirds of his obnoxiousness would vanish. He would remain a nuisance, but he would cease to be a swindler; the injury of having to pay freight on him would cease to be complicated by the insult of being rooked. It is the insult and not the injury that makes the deeper wounds, and causes the greater permanent damage to the national psyche. All of us have been trained, since infancy, in putting up with necessary evils, plainly recognized *as* evils. We know, for example, that the young of the human species commonly smell badly; that garbage men, bootblacks and messenger boys commonly smell worse. These facts are not agreeable, but they remain tolerable because they are universally assumed—because there is no sense of having been tricked and cozened in their perennial discovery. But try to imagine how distressing fatherhood would become if prospective fathers were all taught that the human infant radiates an aroma like the rose—if the truth came constantly as a surprise! Each fresh victim of the deception would feel that he had been basely swindled—that his own child was somehow bogus. Not infrequently, I suppose, he would be tempted to make away with it in some quiet manner, and have another—only to be shocked again. That procedure would be idiotic, admittedly, yet it is exactly the one we follow in politics. At each election we vote in a new set of politicians, insanely assuming that they are better than the set turned out. And at each election we are, as they say in the Motherland, done in.

Of late the fraud has become so gross that the plain people begin to show a great restlessness under it. Like animals in a cage, they trot from one corner to another, endlessly seeking a way out. If the Democrats win one year, it is a pretty sure sign that they will lose the next year. State after State becomes doubtful, pivotal, skittish; even the solid South begins to break. In the cities it is still worse. An evil circle is formed. First the poor taxpayers, robbed by the politicians of one great party and then by those of the other, turn to a group of free-lance rogues in the middle ground—non-partisan candidates, Liberals, reformers or what not: the name is unimportant. Then, flayed and pillaged by these gentry as they never were by the old-time professionals, they go back in despair to the latter, and are flayed and pillaged again. Back to Bach! Back to Tammany! Tammany reigns in New York because the Mitchel outfit was found to be intolerable—in other words, because the reformers were found to be even worse than the professionals. Is the fact surprising? Why should it be? Reformers and professionals are alike politicians in search of jobs; both are trying to bilk the taxpayers. Neither ever has any other motive. If any genuinely honest and altruistic politician had come to the surface in America in my time I'd have heard of him, for I have always frequented newspaper offices, and in a newspaper office the news of such a marvel would cause a dreadful tumult. I can recall no such tumult. The unanimous opinion of all the journalists that I know, excluding a few Liberals who are obviously somewhat balmy—they all believed, for example, that the late war would end war,—is that, since the days of the national Thors and Wotans, no politician who was not out for himself, and for himself alone, has ever drawn the breath of life in the United States.

The gradual disintegration of Liberalism among us, in fact, offers an excellent proof of the truth of my thesis. The Liberals have come to grief by fooling their customers, not merely once too often, but a hundred times too often. Over and over again they have trotted out some new hero, usually from the great open spaces, only to see him taken in the immemorial malpractises within ten days. Their graveyard, indeed, is filled with cracked and upset headstones, many covered with ribald pencilings. Every time there is a scandal in the grand manner the Liberals lose almost as many general officers as either the Democrats or Republicans. Of late, racked beyond endurance by such catastrophes at home, they have gone abroad for their principal heroes; losing humor as well as hope, they now ask us to venerate such astounding paladins as the Hon. Bela Kun, a gentleman who, in any American State, would not only be in the calaboose, but actually in the deathhouse. But this absurdity is only an offshoot of a deeper one. Their primary error lies in making the false assumption that some politicians are better than others. This error they share with the whole American people.

I propose that it be renounced, and contend that

its renunciation would greatly rationalize and improve our politics.   I do not argue that there would
be any improvement in our politicians; on the contrary, I believe that they would remain substantially
as they are today, and perhaps grow even worse.
But what I do argue is that recognizing them frankly
for what they are would instantly and automatically
dissipate the indignation caused by their present
abominations, and that the disappearance of this indignation would promote the public contentment and
happiness.   Under my scheme there would be no more
false assumptions and no more false hopes, and hence
no more painful surprises, no more bitter resentment
of fraud, no more despair.   Politicians, in so far as
they remained necessary, would be kept at work—
but not with any insane notion that they were arch-
angels.   Their rascality would be assumed and discounted, as the rascality of the police is now assumed
and discounted.   Machinery would be gradually developed to limit it and counteract it.   In the end, it
might be utilized in some publicly profitable manner,
as the insensitiveness to filth of garbage men is now
utilized, as the reverence of the clergy for capitalism
is now utilized.   The result, perhaps, would be a
world no better than the present one, but it would at
least be a world more intelligent.

In all this I sincerely hope that no one will mistake me for one who shares the indignation I have

spoken of—that is, for one who believes that politicians can be made good, and cherishes a fond scheme for making them so. I believe nothing of the sort. On the contrary, I am convinced that the art and mystery they practise is essentially and incurably anti-social—that they must remain irreconcilable enemies of the common weal until the end of time. But I maintain that this fact, in itself, is not a bar to their employment. There are, under Christian civilization, many necessary offices that demand the possession of anti-social talents. A professional soldier, regarded realistically, is much worse than a professional politician, for he is a professional murderer and kidnaper, whereas the politician is only a professional sharper and sneak-thief. A clergyman, too, begins to shrink and shrivel on analysis; the work he does in the world is basically almost indistinguishable from that of an astrologer, a witch-doctor or a fortune-teller. He pretends falsely that he can get sinners out of hell, and collects money from them on that promise, tacit or express. If he had to go before a jury with that pretension it would probably go hard with him. But we do not send him before a jury; we grant him his hocus-pocus on the ground that it is necessary to his office, and that his office is necessary to civilization, so-called. I pass over the journalist delicately; the time has not come to turn State's evidence. Suffice it to say that he, too, would probably wither under a stiff cross-examination. If he is no murderer, like the soldier, then he is at least a sharper and swindler, like the politician.

What I plead for, if I may borrow a term in disrepute, is simply *Realpolitik, i. e.,* realism in politics. I can imagine a political campaign purged of all the current false assumptions and false pretenses—a campaign in which, on election day, the voters went to the polls clearly informed that the choice between them was not between an angel and a devil, a good man and a bad man, an altruist and a go-getter, but between two frank go-getters, the one, perhaps, excelling at beautiful and nonsensical words and the other at silent and prehensile deeds—the one a chautauqua orator and the other a porch-climber. There would be, in that choice, something candid, free and exhilarating. Buncombe would be adjourned. The voter would make his selection in the full knowledge of all the facts, as he makes his selection between two heads of cabbage, or two evening papers, or two brands of chewing tobacco. Today he chooses his rulers as he buys bootleg whiskey, never knowing precisely what he is getting, only certain that it is not what it pretends to be. The Scotch may turn out to be wood alcohol or it may turn out to be gasoline; in either case it is not Scotch. How much better if it were plainly labelled, for wood alcohol and gasoline both have their uses—higher uses, indeed, than Scotch. The danger is that the swindled and poisoned consumer, despairing of ever avoiding them when he doesn't want them, may prohibit them even when he does want them, and actually enforce his own prohibition. The danger is that the hopeless voter, forever victimized by his false assumption about politicians, may in the end gather such ferocious indignation that he will abolish them teetotally and at one insane swoop, and so cause government by the people, for the people and with the people to perish from this earth.

VII. FROM A CRITIC'S
NOTEBOOK

1

Progress

THE most important change that has come over
American literature in my time is this: that
American satire, which once aimed all of its
shafts at the relatively civilized minority, now aims
most of them at the imbecile majority. If a satirist
of today undertook to poke fun at the paintings of
Titian and the music of Richard Wagner, he would
be dismissed at once as a clown strayed in from the
barber-shop weeklies and the chautauquas. Yet
Mark Twain did both, and to great applause. To
Mark, for all his humor, there was little that was
ridiculous in such American go-getters as George F.
Babbitt. He looked upon one of them, Henry H.
Rogers, as his best friend, and he made another the
hero of "A Connecticut Yankee." What amused
Mark most profoundly was precisely whatever was
most worthy of sober admiration—sound art, good
manners, the aristocratic ideal. And he was typical

of his age. The satirists of the present age, though they may be less accomplished workmen, are at all events more civilized men. What they make fun of is not what is dignified, or noble, or beautiful, but what is shoddy, and ignoble, and ugly.

2

The Iconoclast

Of a piece with the absurd pedagogical demand for so-called constructive criticism is the doctrine that an iconoclast is a hollow and evil fellow unless he can prove his case. Why, indeed, should he prove it? Doesn't he prove enough when he proves by his blasphemy that this or that idol is defectively convincing—that at least *one* visitor to the shrine is left full of doubts? The fact is enormously significant; it indicates that instinct has somehow risen superior to the shallowness of logic, the refuge of fools. The pedant and the priest have always been the most expert of logicians—and the most diligent disseminators of nonsense and worse. The liberation of the human mind has never been furthered by such learned dunderheads; it has been furthered by gay fellows who heaved dead cats into sanctuaries and then went roistering down the highways of the world, proving to all men that doubt, after all, was safe—

that the god in the sanctuary was finite in his power, and hence a fraud. One horse-laugh is worth ten thousand syllogisms. It is not only more effective; it is also vastly more intelligent.

3

The Artists' Model

The doctrine that art is an imitation of nature is full of folly. Nine-tenths of all the art that one encounters in this world is actually an imitation of other art. Fully a half of it is an imitation twice, thrice or ten times removed. The artist, in fact, is seldom an accurate observer of nature; he leaves that gross and often revolting exploration to geologists, engineers and anatomists. The last thing he wants to see is a beautiful woman in the bright, pitiless sunlight.

4

The Good Citizen as Artist

Again, there is the bad author who defends his manufacture of magazine serials and movie scenarios on the ground that he has a wife, and is in honor bound to support her. I have seen a few such wives.

I dispute the obligation. . . . As for the biological by-products of this fidelity, I rate them even lower. Show me 100 head of ordinary children who are worth one "Heart of Darkness," and I'll subside. As for "Lord Jim," I would not swap it for all the children born in Trenton, N. J., since the Spanish War.

5

Definitive Judgments

The doctrine that every critic worth reading is primarily an artist—that his fundamental aim is not to ascertain the truth, or to mete out justice, or to defend the maxims of Aristotle, or the Ten Commandments, or the statutes of the Harvard Corporation, or the Harrison Anti-Narcotic Act, or the Mann Act—this doctrine seems to give a great deal of offense to pedagogues, and every time one of them mentions it he mourns. Always he makes the accusation that it relieves the critic of his most important duty, to wit, the duty of telling his readers what the thing he criticizes is, and how far it carries out its pretension, and how it relates itself to other things in the same category, or presumably in the same category. The answer here, of course, is that no such duty exists. Its existence, indeed, is no more than a delusion of pedagogues, who invariably labor under the notion that they have said something about this or that when they have given it a name. That delusion is responsible for all of the so-called "criticism" that pedagogues write—the heavy, soggy essays upon Matthew Arnold, Poe as a poet, Browning as a philosopher, the Pre-Raphaelites, Henley, Schiller, Ibsen, Whitman, Milton, Herrick, Molière—in brief, all the blowsy efforts to reach "definite judgments" that such tedious wind-jammers delight in.   What is accomplished by such "definitive judgments"?   Absolutely nothing.   A hedge Lowell's elaborate treatise upon Joaquin Miller will never convince any intelligent man that Miller was an important writer, nor will the same professor's effort to fit Ralph Waldo Emerson into the Methodist æsthetic and gnosiology ever stop any intelligent man from reading Emerson for himself, and enjoying him more or less.   Such "criticism" invariably fails of its ostensible purpose.   In so far as it has any validity and significance at all, it is not as jurisprudence but as work of art.   In brief, the pedagogue, when he essays criticism, becomes an artist in spite of himself. As a moral man, of course, he avoids the sin of being a good artist, but nevertheless he is, within the limits set by his superstitions, an artist.

What separates good critics from bad ones is simply the fact that the former are sound enough artists

to make the matter they discuss seem charming. It
is by this route that they induce their readers to look
into it further, and so achieve their function. This
function is not to be confused with the pedagogical.
It is infinitely more urbane and expansive. Dryden
was surely no schoolmaster, even *in petto*, but when
he set down his views about Shakespeare in his beautiful and ingratiating prose he interested more
readers in the Bard than a whole herd of pedagogues
could have mustered, and so, despite the chill that
often got into his enthusiasm, he probably did more
than any other man to rescue the greatest of English
poets from his Restoration days neglect. What a
palpable artist finds interesting is very apt to seem
interesting to all persons of taste and education; what
a mere birchman advocates is apt to arouse their instinctive aversion. They do not want to be told precisely what to think about the thing discussed; all
they want to be told is that it is worth examining.
Every effort to lay down immutable conclusions, to
state impeccable principles, to instruct them in their
moral and æsthetic duties—in other words, every
effort to think for them, as a college tutor thinks for
a sophomore, and a professor for a tutor, and a university president for a professor, and a board of
trustees for a president—is bound to annoy them and
chase them away. Despite all the "definitive judg-

ments" that pedants have pronounced upon Walt Whitman, almost always unfavorably, he continues to live and to grow.   And despite all their herculean efforts to hold up Howells, he is dead.

VIII. TOTENTANZ

I CAN think of no great city of this world (putting aside Rio de Janeiro, Sydney and San Francisco) that is set amid scenes of greater natural beauty than New York, by which I mean, of course, Manhattan. Recall Berlin on its dismal plain, Paris and London on their toy rivers, Madrid on its desert, Copenhagen on its swamp, Rome on its ancient sewer and its absurd little hills, and then glance at Manhattan on its narrow and rock-ribbed island, with deep rivers to either side and the wide bay before it. No wonder its early visitors, however much they denounced the Dutch, always paused to praise the scene! Before it grew up, indeed, New York must have been strangely beautiful. But it was the beauty of freshness and unsophistication—in brief, of youth—and now it is no more. The town today, I think, is quite the ugliest in the world—uglier, even, than Liverpool, Chicago or Berlin. If it were actually beautiful, as London, say, is beautiful, or Munich, or Charleston, or Florence, or even parts of Paris and Washington, then New Yorkers would not be so childishly appreciative of the few so-called beauty spots that it has—

for example, Washington Square, Gramercy Park, Fifth avenue and Riverside drive. Washington Square, save for one short row of old houses on the North side, is actually very shabby and ugly—a blot rather than a beauty spot. The trees, year in and year out, have a mangy and sclerotic air; the grass is like stable litter; the tall tower on the South side is ungraceful and preposterous; the memorial arch is dirty and undignified; the whole place looks dingy, frowsy and forlorn. Compare it to Mt. Vernon Square in Baltimore: the difference is that between a charwoman and a grand lady. As for Gramercy Park, it is celebrated only because it is in New York; if it were in Washington or London it would not attract a glance. Fifth avenue, to me, seems to be showy rather than beautiful. What gives it its distinction is simply its spick and span appearance of wealth; it is the only New York street that ever looks well-fed and clean. Riverside drive lacks even so much; it is second-rate from end to end, and especially where it is gaudiest. What absurd and hideous houses, with their brummagem Frenchiness, their pathetic effort to look aristocratic! What bad landscaping! What grotesque monuments! From its heights the rich look down upon the foul scars of the Palisades, as the rich of Fifth avenue and Central Park West look down upon the anemic grass, bare rocks and blowing newspapers of Central Park.

Alone among the great cities of the East, New York has never developed a domestic architecture of any charm, or, indeed, of any character at all. There are neighborhoods in Boston, in Philadelphia, in Baltimore and in many lesser cities that have all the dignity and beauty of London, but in New York the brownstone mania of the Nineteenth Century brought down the whole town to one level of depressing ugliness, and since brownstone has gone out there has been no development whatever of indigenous design, but only a naïve copying of models—the sky-scraper from Chicago and the dwelling-house from Paris. Along Fifth avenue, from the Fifty-ninth street corner to the upper end of Central Park, there is not a single house that looks reposeful and habitable. Along Park avenue—but Park avenue, for all its flash of creamy brick, is surely one of the most hideous streets in all the world!

But the life of the city, it must be confessed, is as interesting as its physical aspect is dull. It is, even more than London or Paris, the modern Babylon, and since 1914 it has entered upon a period of luxuriousness that far surpasses anything seen on earth since the fall of the Eastern Empire. During many a single week, I daresay, more money is spent in New York upon useless and evil things than would suffice to run the kingdom of Denmark for a year. All the colossal accumulated wealth of the United States, the greatest robber nation in history, tends to force itself at least once a year through the narrow neck of the Manhattan funnel. To that harsh island come all the thieves of the Republic with their loot—bankers from the fat lands of the Middle West, lumbermen from the Northwestern coasts, mine owners from the mountains, oil speculators from Texas and Oklahoma, cotton-mill sweaters from the South, steel magnates and manufacturers from the Black Country, black-legs and exploiters without end—all laden with cash, all eager to spend it, all easy marks for the town rogues and panders. The result is a social organization that ought to be far more attractive to novelists than it is—a society founded upon the prodigious wealth of Monte Cristo and upon the tastes of sailors home from a long voyage. At no time and place in modern times has harlotry reached so delicate and yet so effusive a development; it becomes, in one form or another, one of the leading industries of the town. New York, indeed, is the heaven of every variety of man with something useless and expensive to sell. There come the merchants with their bales, of Persian prayer-rugs, of silk pajamas, of yellow girls, of strange jugs and carboys, of hand-painted oil-paintings, of old books, of gim-cracks and tinsel from all the four corners of the world, and there they find customers waiting in swarms, their check-books open and ready. What town in Christendom has ever supported so many houses of entertainment, so many mimes and mountebanks, so many sharpers and coney-catchers, so many bawds and pimps, so many hat-holders and door-openers, so many miscellaneous servants to idleness and debauchery? The bootlegging industry takes on proportions that are almost unbelievable; there are thousands of New Yorkers, resident and transient, who pay more for alcohol every year than they pay for anything else save women. I have heard of a single party at which the guests drank 100 cases of champagne in an evening—100 cases at $100 a case—and it was, as entertainments go in New York today, a quiet and decorous affair. It is astonishing that no Zola has arisen to describe this engrossing and incomparable dance of death. Upton Sinclair once attempted it, in "The Metropolis," but Sinclair, of course, was too indignant for the job. Moreover, the era he dealt with was mild and amateurish; today the pursuit of sensation has been brought to a far higher degree of perfection. One must go back to the oriental capitals of antiquity to find anything even remotely resembling it. Compared to the revels that go on in New York every night, the carnalities of the West End of Berlin are trivial and childish, and those of Paris and the Côte d'Azure take on the harmless aspect of a Sunday-school picnic.

What will be the end of the carnival? If historical precedent counts for anything, it will go on to catastrophe. But what sort of catastrophe? I hesitate to venture upon a prophecy. Manhattan Island, with deep rivers all around it, seems an almost ideal scene for a great city revolution, but I doubt very much that there is any revolutionary spirit in its proletariat. Some mysterious enchantment holds its workers to their extraordinarily uncomfortable life; they apparently get a vague sort of delight out of the great spectacle that they are no part of. The New York workman patronizes fellow workmen from the provinces even more heavily than the Wall Street magnate patronizes country mortgage-sharks. He is excessively proud of his citizenship in the great metropolis, though all it brings him is an upper berth in a dog kennel. Riding along the elevated on the East Side and gaping into the windows of the so-called human habitations that stretch on either hand, I often wonder what process of reasoning impels, say, a bricklayer or a truckdriver to spend his days in such vile hutches. True enough, he is paid a few dollars more a week in New York than he would receive anywhere else, but he gets little more use out of them than an honest bank teller. In almost any other large American city he would have a much better house to live in, and better food; in the smaller towns his advantage would be very considerable. Moreover, his chance of lifting himself out of slavery to some measure of economic independence and autonomy would be greater anywhere else; if it is hard for the American workman everywhere to establish a business of his own, it is triply hard in New York, where rents are killingly high and so much capital is required to launch a business that only Jews can raise it. Nevertheless, the poor idiot hangs on to his coop, dazzled by the wealth and splendor on display all around him. His susceptibility to this lure makes me question his capacity for revolution. He is too stupid and poltroonish for it, and he has too much respect for money. It is this respect for money in the proletariat, in fact, that chiefly safeguards and buttresses capitalism in America. It is secure among us because Americans venerate it too much to attack it.

What will finish New York in the end, I suppose, will be an onslaught from without, not from within. The city is the least defensible of great capitals. Give an enemy command of the sea, and he will be able to take it almost as easily as he could take Copenhagen. It has never been attacked in the past, indeed, without being taken. The strategists of the General Staff at Washington seem to be well aware of this fact, for their preparations to defend the city from a foe afloat have always been half-hearted and lacking in confidence. Captain Stuart Godfrey, U. S. A., who contributes the note on the fortifications of the port to Fremont Rider's "New York City: A Guide to Travelers," is at pains to warn his lay readers that the existing forts protect only the narrow spaces in front of them—that "they cannot be expected to prevent the enemy from landing elsewhere," *e. g.*, anywhere along the long reaches of the Long Island coast.   Once such a landing were effected, the fact that the city stands upon an island, with deep water behind it, would be a handicap rather than a benefit.   If it could not be taken and held, it could at least be battered to pieces, and so made untenable. The guns of its own forts, indeed, might be turned upon it, once those forts were open to attack from the rear.   After that, the best the defenders could do would be to retire to the natural bombproofs in the cellars of the Union Hill, N. J., breweries, and there wait for God to deliver them.   They might, of course, be able to throw down enough metal from the Jersey heights to prevent the enemy occupying the city and reopening its theatres and bordellos, but the more successful they were in this enterprise the more cruelly Manhattan would be used.   Altogether, an assault from the sea promises to give the New Yorkers something to think about.

That it will be attempted before many years have come and gone seems to me to be very likely and I have a sneaking fear that it may succeed.   As a veteran of five wars and a life-long student of hom-

icidal science, I am often made uneasy, indeed, by
the almost universal American assumption that no
conceivable enemy could inflict serious wounds upon
the Republic—that the Atlantic Ocean alone, not to
mention the stupendous prowess of *Homo amer-
icanus,* makes it eternally safe from aggression.
This notion has just enough truth in it to make it
dangerous. That the *whole* country could not be
conquered and occupied I grant you, but no intelligent enemy would think for a moment of trying to
conquer it. All that would be necessary to bring
even the most intransigeant patriots to terms would be
to take and hold a small part of it—say the part lying
to the East and North of the general line of the
Potomac river. Early in the late war, when efforts
were under way to scare the American *booboisie* with
the German bugaboo, one of the Allied propagandists
printed a book setting forth plans alleged to have
been made by the German General Staff to land an
army at the Virginia capes, march on Pittsburgh, and
so separate the head of the country from its liver,
kidneys, gizzard, heart, spleen, bladder, lungs and
other lights. The plan was persuasive, but I doubt
that it originated in Potsdam; there was a smell of
Whitehall upon it. One of the things most essential
to its execution, in fact, was left out as it was set
forth, to wit, a thrust southward from Canada to
meet and support the thrust northwestward. But

even this is not necessary.   Any invader who emptied New York and took the line of the Hudson would have Uncle Sam by the tail, and could enter upon peace negotiations with every prospect of getting very polite attention.   The American people, of course, could go on living without New York, but they could not go on living as a great and puissant nation. Steadily, year by year, they have made New York more and more essential to the orderly functioning of the American state.   If it were cut off from the rest of the country the United States would be in the hopeless position of a man relieved of his medulla oblongata—that is to say, of a man without even enough equipment left to be a father, a patriot and a Christian.

Nevertheless, it is highly probable that the pre-destined enemy, when he comes at last, will direct his first and hardest efforts to cutting off New York, and then make some attempt to keep it detached after-ward.   This, in fact, is an essential part of the new higher strategy, which is based upon economic con-siderations, as the old strategy was based upon dy-nastic considerations.   In the Middle Ages, the ob-ject of war was to capture and hamstring a king; at present it is to dismember a great state, and so make it impotent.   The Germans, had they won, would have broken up the British Empire, and probably detached important territories from France, Italy and Russia, beside gobbling Belgium *in toto*. The French, tantalized by a precarious and incomplete victory, attempted to break up Germany, as they broke up Austria. The chances are that an enemy capable of taking and holding New York would never give it back wholly—that is, would never consent to its restoration to the Union on the old terms. What would be proposed, I venture, would be its conversion into a sort of free state—a new Dantzig, perhaps functioning, as now, as the financial and commercial capital of the country, but nevertheless lying outside the bounds politically. This would solve the problem of the city's subsistence, and still enable the conqueror to keep his hold upon it. It is my belief that the New Yorkers, after the first blush of horror, would agree to the new arrangement and even welcome it. Their patriotism, as things stand, is next to nothing. I have never heard, indeed, of a single honest patriot in the whole town; every last man who even pretends to kiss the flag is simply a swindler with something to sell. This indifference to the great heart-throbs of the hinterland is not to be dismissed as mere criminality; it is founded upon the plain and harsh fact that New York is alien to the rest of the country, not only in blood and tastes, but also in fundamental interests—that the sort of life that New Yorkers lead differs radically from the sort of life that the rest of the American people lead,

and that their deepest instincts vary with it. The
city, in truth, already constitutes an independent free
state in all save the name. The ordinary American
law does not run there, save when it has been specifically ratified, and the ordinary American *mores* are
quite unknown there. What passes as virtue in
Kansas is regarded as intolerable vice in New York,
and *vice versa*. The town is already powerful
enough to swing the whole country when it wants to,
as it did on the war issue in 1917, but the country is
quite impotent to swing the town. Every great wave
of popular passion that rolls up on the prairies is
dashed to spray when it strikes the hard rocks of
Manhattan.

As a free state, licensed to prey upon the hinterland but unharassed by its Crô-Magnon prejudices
and delusions, New York would probably rise to
heights of very genuine greatness, and perhaps become the most splendid city known to history. For
one thing, it would be able, once it had cut the painter,
to erect barriers and conditions around the privilege
of citizenship, and so save itself from the double
flood that now swamps it—first, of broken-down
peasants from Europe, and secondly and more important, of fugitive rogues from all the land West
and South of the Hudson. Citizenship in New York
is now worth no more than citizenship in Arkansas,
for it is open to any applicant from the marshes of

Bessarabia, and, still worse, to any applicant from Arkansas. The great city-states of history have been far more fastidious. Venice, Antwerp, London, the Hansa towns, Carthage, Tyre, Cnossus, Alexandria— they were all very sniffish. Rome began to wobble when the Roman franchise was extended to immigrants from the Italian hill country, *i. e.*, the Arkansas of that time. The Hansa towns, under the democracy that has been forced upon them, are rapidly sinking to the level of Chicago and Philadelphia. New York, free to put an end to this invasion, and to drive out thousands of the gorillas who now infest it—more, free from the eternal blackmail of laws made at Albany and the Methodist tyranny of laws made at Washington—could face the future with resolution and security, and in the course of a few generations it might conceivably become genuinely civilized. It would still stand as toll-taker on the chief highway of American commerce; it would still remain the premier banker and usurer of the Republic. But it would be loosed from the bonds which now tend so strenuously to drag it down to the level of the rest of the country. Free at last, it could cease to be the auction-room and bawdy-house that it is now, and so devote its brains and energy to the building up of a civilization.

IX. MEDITATIONS IN THE
METHODIST DESERT

1

The New Galahad

MY agents in attendance upon the so-called moving pictures tell me that persons who frequent such shows begin to tire of Western films—that they are no longer roused to clapper-clawing by the spectacle of actors in patent-leather jack-boots murdering Indians and Mexicans. Several of the astute Ashkenazim in charge of the movie industry, noting that slackening of taste, have sought to find a new hero to replace the scout and cowboy, but so far without success. The children of today, young and old, seem to take no interest in pirates, nor are they stirred by train-robbers, safe-blowers and other such illicit adventurers. It can't be that the movie censorship is to blame, for the same thing is visible in the field of *belles lettres*. The dime novel, once so prosperous, is practically dead. The great deeds of the James brothers, known to every literate boy in my youth, are now forgotten. And so

are the great deeds of Nick Carter and Old Sleuth:
the detective has fallen with his prey.

What is needed, obviously, is a new hero for the
infantry of the land, for if one is not quickly supplied
there is some danger that the boys will begin ad-
miring Y. M. C. A. secretaries, crooked members of
the Cabinet and lecturers on sex hygiene. In this
emergency I nominate the bootlegger—not, of course,
the abject scoundrel who peddles bogus Scotch in
clubs and office buildings, but the dashing, romantic,
defiant fellow who brings the stuff up from the Spanish Main. He is, indeed, almost an ideal hero. He
is the true heir, not only of the old-time Indian
fighters and train-robbers, but also of the tough and
barnacled deep-water sailors, now no more. He
faces the perils of the high seas in a puny shallop,
and navigates the worst coast in the world in contempt
of wind and storm. Think of him lying out there on
wild nights in Winter, with the waves piling mountain-
high and the gale standing his crazy little craft on
her beam! Think of him creeping in in his motor-
boat on Christmas Eve, risking his life that the
greatest of Christian festivals may be celebrated in a
Christian and respectable manner! Think of him
soaked and freezing, facing his exile and its hard-
ships uncomplainingly, saving his money that his old
mother may escape the poor-farm, that his wife may
have her operation for gall-stones, that his little chil-

dren may be decently fed and clad, and go to school regularly, and learn the principles of Americanism!

This brave lad is not only the heir of Jesse James and Ned Buntline; he is also the heir of John Hancock and of all the other heroes who throttled the accursed Hun in 1776. All the most gallant among them were smugglers, and in their fragile craft they brought in, not only rum, but also liberty. The Revolution was not only against the person of the Potsdam tyrant, George III; it was also, and especially, against harsh and intolerable laws—the worst of them the abhorrent Stamp Act. But was the Stamp Act worse than Prohibition? I leave it to any fair man. Prohibition, in fact, is a hundred times as foul, false, oppressive and tyrannical. If the Stamp Act was worth a Revolution, the Prohibition is worth a massacre and an earthquake. Well, it has already bred its Hancocks, and soon or late, no doubt, it will breed its Molly Pitchers, Paul Reveres and Mad Anthony Waynes. Liberty, driven from the land by the Methodist White Terror, has been given a refuge by the hardy boys of the Rum Fleet. In their bleak and lonely exile they cherish her and keep her alive. Some day, let us hope, they will storm the coast, slit the gullets of her enemies, and restore her to her dominion. The lubbers of the land have limber necks; their blood runs pale and yellow. But on the roaring deep there are still men who are colossally he, and when the bugle calls they will not fail.

2

Optimist vs. Optimist

If these heroes *do* fail, alas, alas, then all will be lost, including honor. For there is not the slightest sign of revolt among the craven hordes who cling to the land, ignominiously dependent for their very existence as Christians upon the gallant fellows beyond the twelve-mile limit. They simply go on hoping against hope. Each successive Congress is to relieve them, rescue them, restore the liberties bequeathed to them by the Fathers. And each successive Congress does nothing of the kind. Nor, I believe, will any one coming hereafter. Congress is made up eternally of petty scoundrels, pusillanimous poltroons, highly vulnerable and cowardly men: they will never risk provoking the full fire of the Anti-Saloon League. The notion that such degraded fellows will ever rise up and put down Prohibition, so fondly cherished by the wets, is thus a snare and a mocking, and so is the notion that they will presently find a way to enforce it, cherished by the drys. Optimist eat optimist! As for me, I can find no reason whatever for believing that, within the lifetime of men now living, the voluptuous consumption of alcohol will be countenanced by law in the Republic, and neither do I see any reason for believing that it will ever be stopped, nor, indeed, any reason for believing that any serious effort will be made to stop it.

It is commonly argued by the more impatient and worthy opponents of the Methodist millennium that the Eighteenth Amendment was slipped through Congress and the State legislatures against the wishes of the majority of American freemen—that the thing was accomplished by a sort of trick, partly political and partly magical. It is further argued that, had the soldiers who were then abroad, fighting for human liberty, been at home and voting, they would have piled up such majorities for wet candidates that both Houses of Congress would have been made proof against the Anti-Saloon League. It seems to me that both contentions are unsound. The Eighteenth Amendment, when it was passed, actually had a majority behind it, and I incline to think that that majority was a very substantial one. What made it so large was simply the war hysteria of the time. *Homo boobiens* was scientifically rowelled and run amok with the news that all the German brewers of the country were against the amendment; he observed himself that all German sympathizers, whether actual

Germans or not, were bitter opponents of it. His nights made dreadful by dreams of German spies, he was willing to do anything to put them down, and one of the things he was willing to do was to swallow Prohibition. When he recovered from his terror, it was too late; the first article of the Methodist Book of Discipline had been read into the Constitution, and there it remains today, an unpleasant fly in imperishable amber. The soldiers, had they been at home, would have gone the way of their lay brothers. They were, if anything, even more in terror of Germans than the latter, and even more eager to floor them and so get rid of them. In every camp and cantonment Y. M. C. A. secretaries addressed the conscripts daily, instructing them in the moral nature of the crusade they were engaged in. The effects are visible today in the familiar swineries of the American Legion; its members are still down with the war psychosis. Moreover, it is not to be forgotten that large numbers of soldiers could not have voted, even if they had been at home. For example, those who were minors. Again, the Southern Negroes. Yet again, the enormous number of aliens who were rushed to the trenches by the draft boards to relieve native patriots—in New York City alone, fully 25,000, most of them Russian Jews. Finally, it is to be recalled that there was no plebiscite on Prohibition—that the men who put it into the Constitution were all safely in office at the time the test suddenly confronted them.

But what of the state of public opinion today? Isn't it a fact that hundreds of thousands of persons who were in favor of Prohibition in 1919 are now so disgusted by its colossal failure that they have turned violently against it? I doubt it. I know of no such person. I know of a great many persons who, though they voted for Prohibition when they had the chance, or, at all events, favored it, now guzzle like actors or policemen, but I believe that substantially all of them, if the thing were put up to them tomorrow, would be for it again. Whoever believes that they have changed heart is a very poor student of the Puritan psyche. What a Puritan advocates and what he does have no necessary connection. The late Anthony Comstock was a diligent collector of dirty books, and used to entertain favored callers by exhibiting his worst specimens to them. Nevertheless, Comstock was honestly in favor of suppressing such books, and would have gone to the extreme length of giving up his own recreation if he had ever been convinced that it would have helped the cause. To the Puritan, indeed, moral obligation is something quite outside personal conduct, and has very little contact with it. He may be, in private, an extremely gross and porcine fellow, and he frequently is, but that fact doesn't diminish his veneration for his ethical ideal in the slightest. Brought to the mark, he always sticks to that ideal, however absurdly his conduct clashes with it. As everyone knows, he is rather more prone than most other men to commit fornication, particularly in its more sordid and degrading forms; nevertheless, it is impossible to imagine him advocating any relaxation of the prevailing sexual taboos, however beneficial it would be. Again, as everyone also knows, he is very apt, when he drinks at all, to make a hog of himself, for the amiable drinking customs of civilized men are beyond him; nevertheless, it is impossible to imagine him admitting specifically that any man has a right to drink at all. This last fact explains something that often puzzles foreign observers: the relative smallness and impotence of anti-Prohibition organizations in America, despite the great amount of gabbling against Prohibition that goes on. It is due to the Puritan's fear of appearing on the side of the devil. He will drink in private, but he will not defend the practise in public.

It thus seems to me that so long as Puritanism remains the dominant philosophy in America—and certainly it shows no sign of relaxing its hold upon the low-caste Anglo-Saxon majority—it will be quite hopeless to look for an abandonment of Prohibition, or even for any relaxation of its extravagant and

probably unconstitutional excesses. But for precisely the same reason it seems to me to be very un-
likely that Prohibition will ever be enforced, or,
indeed, that any honest effort will ever be made to
enforce it. For the Puritan's enthusiasm for the
moral law is always grounded, at least in large part,
upon a keen realization that it is, after all, only an
ideal—that it may be evaded whenever the tempta-
tion grows strong enough—that he himself may evade
it, readily and safely. Like every other man, he
likes to kick up now and then, and forget his holiest
principles. He achieves this kicking up by sinning.
When drinking was perfectly lawful, he got no
pleasure out of it and so tried to put it down, but
now that it is against the law he delights in it, and so
long as he delights in it he will keep on doing it. If
the Seventh Commandment were repealed tomorrow,
military marriages would decrease 95 per cent. in
rural America, and the great hotels at Atlantic City
would be given over to the bats and owls. Let us,
therefore, neither delude ourselves nor get into sweats
of Puritan-like fear. Prohibition officers will continue to beat the land for stills and bribes until you
and I are long gone and forgotten, and bootleggers
will continue to elude them. No genuinely wet President will be elected, save by accident, in our time,
and no President will ever be able to enforce Prohibition. Respect for the Constitution will be heard of in

every campaign, and then it will be forgotten for four years more. It will give candidates something to talk about, but it will not give the rest of us anything to worry about.

3

Caveat for the Defense

The wets, I often think, are worse frauds than the drys. For example, consider their great current eagerness to assure everyone that they are absolutely against the saloon—that they would not revive it for an instant, even if they could. All of their spokesmen stop short dramatically after demanding the restoration of light wines and beer; they are virtuously opposed, it would appear, to all forms of hard liquor, as they are opposed to the saloon. In this position I can detect nothing respectable. Either the advocates of it are hypocrites trying to fool the Prohibitionists with pious protestations, or they have been themselves corrupted by Methodist superstitions. The plain fact is, of course, that the saloon, at its worst, was a great deal better than any of the substitutes that have grown up under Prohibition—nay, that it was a great deal better than the ideal substitutes imagined by the Prohibitionists: for example, the Y. M. C. A. And it must be equally plain that

light wines and beer would not always satisfy the
yearning of the normal man for alcoholic refresh-
ment—that there are times when his system, if he is
sound in body, craves far stronger stuff. To say
that such a normal man, at five o'clock in the afternoon, wants to drink a *Humpen* of beer, or that, on a
cold Winter morning, his inner urge would be met by
half a bottle of Pontet Canet is to say something so
absurd that the mere statement of it is sufficient
refutation. The fact is, of course, that the last
chance to exile hard liquors for light wines and beer
went glimmering when the Eighteenth Amendment
was ratified. In 1918, perhaps, the scheme had a
certain plausibility, for the American consumption
of spirits had been declining for years, and very good
beer, imported from Germany and Bohemia, was
everywhere obtainable at low prices, and the use of
wine, chiefly because of the influence of Italian res-
taurants and the propaganda of the California vine-
growers, was rapidly increasing. But the years of
Prohibition have reconverted Americans into a nation
of whiskey and gin drinkers, as they were before the
Germans brought in lager beer in the fifties of the
last century. Light wines and beer, I believe, would
not satisfy them now, even at meals; there would be
just as much bootlegging under a modified Volstead
Act as there is today. Prohibition has restored the
hard guzzling of Daniel Webster's day.

As for the saloon, the case against it, as voiced by both Prohibitionists and anti-Prohibitionists, is chiefly based upon a recollection of what the thing was at its lowest and worst, which is just as sensible as arguing against Christianity on the ground that a certain minority of the rev. clergy are notorious swine. The utterly vicious saloons were always relatively rare, even along the waterfront, and an honest execution of the laws in force before Prohibition would have exterminated them in ten days. Their existence was a proof, not that the saloon itself was inherently evil, but simply that it could be made evil by corrupt government. To blame it for that fact would be like blaming the Constitution for the fact that Federal judges habitually violate it. The normal saloon, I am convinced, was not an evil influence in its vicinage, but a good one. It not only enabled the poor man to effect that occasional escape from wife and children which every man must make if he would remain sane; it also threw him into a society palpably better than that of his home or his workshop, and accustomed him to refinements which unquestionably improved him. The conversation of a precinct leader or of a brewery collector would make but little impression, I daresay, in the Century Club, on the Harvard campus or in the cloakrooms of the United States Senate, but in the average saloon of a poor neighborhood it took on an unmistakable dignity and authority.   This collector (or *Todsäufer,* as he was called) had fresh news; he was a man of comparatively large affairs; he had an air about him of the great world; most important of all, he was professionally communicative and affable.   The influence of such a man upon the customers of the place, all of whom were bidden to drink and permitted to converse with him, was necessarily for the good.   He was, in every sense comprehensible to them, a better man than they were.   He had the use of more money; he dressed better; he knew more; he couched his ideas in subtler and more graceful terms; he was better bathed and had better table manners.   The effect of his visits, though perhaps not as massive, was comparable to the effect that would have been worked by visits by, say, Bishop Manning or Dr. Nicholas Murray Butler.   In his presence discussion took on a higher tone, and he left behind him, in many a simple heart, an aspiration toward nobler things.

But it was not only the *Todsäufer* who was a missionary of light and a pattern of the amenities; so also was the saloon itself.   It represented the only concept of beauty and dignity that ever entered into the lives of many of its customers.   Surrounded all day by the inconceivable hideousness of the American workshop, and confronted on their return from work by the depressing ugliness of homes outfitted out of

department-stores and on the instalment plan, with
slatternly women and filthy children as the fauna of
the scene, they found themselves, in the saloon, in
a markedly superior milieu. Here some regard was
given to æsthetics. Here was relatively pretentious
architecture. Here were polished hardwoods, re-
splendent mirrors, comfortable chairs, glittering
glassware and metals, innumerable small luxuries.
Here, above all, was an attempt at genuine cleanliness. The poor saloons of the by-streets were not
to be compared, of course, to the superb drinking-
rooms of the great hotels, but they were at least much
cleaner than any of the homes or factories surrounding them, and they were at least more beautiful than
the adjacent livery-stables, cigar-stores, barber-shops
and Methodist Little Bethels. Furthermore, they set
forth an example of life upon a more urbane and
charming scale. Men had to be more polite in
saloons than they were at home; if they were not,
they ran risks of colliding with the fists of their
fellow patrons and with the bartender's Excaliburs,
the bung-starter and ice-pick. The braggart and
bully here met his quick doom; the unsocial fellow
felt the weight of public disapproval; the ignoramus
learned the bitter taste of sniffs and sneers. Life was
more spacious spiritually and more luxurious physically. Instead of the nicked chinaware of his home
the customer encountered shining glass; instead of

spitting out of the window or on the floor he discharged himself into magnificent brass spittoons or
into the brook that ran under the bar-rail; instead of
the ghastly fried beefsteaks and leathery delicatessen
of his wife's cuisine, he ate appetizing herring, delicate *Wienerwürste*, well-devised *Kartoffelsalat*, cel-
ery, olives, and even such exotic titbits as *Blutwurst*,
Pumpernickel, *Bohnensalat* and caviare.

To argue that such luxuries and amenities had no
effect is to argue utter nonsense. I believe fully
that the rise of the latter-day saloon (a product of
the financing of saloonkeepers by wealthy brewers,
so much denounced by superficial sociologists) had
a very benign effect upon American manners. It
purged the city workmen of their old boorish-
ness and pugnacity; it taught them the difference
between mere fodder and civilized food; it shamed
them into a certain cleanliness; it gave them some
dim comprehension of design and ornamentation.
In more than one American city the influence of the
saloon is visible today in ecclesiastical architecture,
and everywhere it is visible in theatre architecture.
I name one thing specifically: the use of polished
hardwoods. The first parquetry ever seen in America was in saloons. And so was the first tile-work.
And so was the first plate-glass. Where the saloon
reached its highest development there American life
became richest and most expansive. The clatter

against it is ignorant, unfair, philistine and disingenuous.

4

Portrait of an Ideal World

That alcohol in dilute aqueous solution, when taken into the human organism, acts as a depressant, not as a stimulant, is now so much a commonplace of knowledge that even the more advanced varieties of physiologists are beginning to be aware of it. The intelligent layman no longer resorts to the jug when he has important business before him, whether intellectual or manual; he resorts to it after his business is done, and he desires to release his taut nerves and reduce the steam-pressure in his spleen. Alcohol, so to speak, unwinds us. It raises the threshold of sensation and makes us less sensitive to external stimuli, and particularly to those that are unpleasant. It reduces and simplifies the emotions. Putting a brake upon all the qualities which enable us to get on in the world and shine before our fellows—for example, combativeness, shrewdness, diligence, ambition,—it releases the qualities which mellow us and make our fellows love us—for example, amiability, generosity, toleration, humor, sympathy. A man who has taken aboard two or three cocktails is less competent than he was before to steer a battleship down the Ambrose Channel, or to cut off a leg, or to draw up a deed of trust, or to conduct Bach's B minor mass, but he is immensely more competent to entertain a dinner party, or to admire a pretty girl, or to *hear* Bach's B minor mass. The harsh, useful things of the world, from pulling teeth to digging potatoes, are best done by men who are as starkly sober as so many convicts in the death-house, but the lovely and useless things, the charming and exhilarating things, are best done by men with, as the phrase is, a few sheets in the wind. *Pithecanthropus erectus* was a teetotaler, but the angels, you may be sure, know what is proper at 5 P. M.

All this is so obvious that I marvel that no utopian has ever proposed to abolish all the sorrows of the world by the simple device of getting and keeping the whole human race gently stewed. I do not say drunk, remember; I say simply gently stewed—and apologize, as in duty bound, for not knowing how to describe the state in a more seemly phrase. The man who is in it is a man who has put all of his best qualities into his showcase. He is not only immensely more amiable than the cold sober man; he is immeasurably more decent. He reacts to all situations in an expansive, generous and humane manner. He has become more liberal, more tolerant, more kind. He is a better citizen, husband, father, friend. The enterprises that make human life on this earth uncomfortable and unsafe are never launched by such men. They are not makers of wars; they do not rob and oppress anyone; they invent no such plagues as high tariffs, 100 per cent. Americanism and Prohibition. All the great villainies of history, from the murder of Abel to the Treaty of Versailles, have been perpetrated by sober men, and chiefly by tee-totalers. But all the charming and beautiful things, from the Song of Songs to terrapin *à la* Maryland, and from the nine Beethoven symphonies to the Martini cocktail, have been given to humanity by men who, when the hour came, turned from well water to something with color to it, and more in it than mere oxygen and hydrogen.

I am well aware, of course, that getting the whole human race stewed and keeping it stewed, year in and year out, would present formidable technical difficulties. It would be hard to make the daily dose of each individual conform exactly to his private needs, and hard to get it to him at precisely the right time. On the one hand there would be the constant danger that large minorities might occasionally become cold sober, and so start wars, theological disputes, moral reforms, and other such unpleasantnesses. On the other hand, there would be danger that other

minorities might proceed to actual intoxication, and
so annoy us all with their fatuous bawling or maudlin
tears. But such technical obstacles, of course, are by
no means insurmountable. Perhaps they might be got
around by abandoning the administration of alcohol
per ora and distributing it instead by impregnat-
ing the air with it. I throw out the suggestion,
and pass on. Such questions are for men skilled
in therapeutics, government and business efficiency.
They exist today and their enterprises often show a
high ingenuity, but, being chiefly sober, they devote
too much of their time to harassing the rest of us.
Half-stewed, they would be ten times as humane, and
perhaps at least half as efficient. Thousands of
them, relieved of their present anti-social duties,
would be idle, and eager for occupation. I trust to
them in this small matter. If they didn't succeed
completely, they would at least succeed partially.

The objection remains that even small doses of
alcohol, if each followed upon the heels of its
predecessor before the effects of the latter had worn
off, would have a deleterious effect upon the physical health of the race—that the death-rate would
increase, and whole categories of human beings
would be exterminated. The answer here is that
what I propose is not lengthening the span of life,
but augmenting its joys. Suppose we assume that
its duration is reduced 20 per cent. My reply is that

its delights will be increased at least 100 per cent. Misled by statisticians, we fall only too often into the error of worshiping mere figures. To say that A will live to be eighty and B will die at forty is certainly not to argue plausibly that A is more to be envied than B. A, in point of fact, may have to spend all of his eighty years in Kansas or Arkansas, with nothing to eat save corn and hog-meat and nothing to drink save polluted river water, whereas B may put in his twenty years of discretion upon the Côte d'Azure, *wie Gott im Frankreich*. It is my contention that the world I picture, even assuming the average duration of human life to be cut down 50 per cent., would be an infinitely happier and more charming world than that we live in today—that no intelligent human being, having once tasted its peace and joy, would go back voluntarily to the harsh brutalities and stupidities that we now suffer, and idiotically strive to prolong. If intelligent Americans, in these depressing days, still cling to life and try to stretch it out longer and longer, it is surely not logically, but only atavistically. It is the primeval brute in them that hangs on, not the man. The man knows only too well that ten years in a genuinely civilized and happy country would be infinitely better than a geological epoch under the curses he must face and endure every day.

Moreover, there is no need to admit that the mod-

erate alcoholization of the whole race would materially reduce the duration of life. A great many
of us are moderately alcoholized already, and yet
manage to survive quite as long as the blue-noses.
As for the blue-noses themselves, who would repine
if breathing alcohol-laden air brought them down
with delirium tremens and so sterilized and exterminated them?   The advantage to the race in general would be obvious and incalculable. All the
worst strains—which now not only persist, but even
prosper—would be stamped out in a few generations, and so the average human being would move
appreciably away from, say, the norm of a Baptist
clergyman in Georgia and toward the norm of
Shakespeare, Mozart and Goethe. It would take
aeons, of course, to go all the way, but there would
be progress with every generation, slow but sure.
Today, it must be manifest, we make no progress
at all; instead we slip steadily backward. That
the average civilized man of today is inferior to the
average civilized man of two or three generations
ago is too plain to need arguing. He has less enterprise and courage; he is less resourceful and various;
he is more like a rabbit and less like a lion. Harsh
oppressions have made him what he is. He is the
victim of tyrants. . . . Well, no man with two or
three cocktails in him is a tyrant. He may be
foolish, but he is not cruel. He may be noisy, but

he is also genial, tolerant, generous and kind. My proposal would restore Christianity to the world. It would rescue mankind from moralists, pedants and brutes.

X. ESSAY IN CONSTRUCTIVE CRITICISM

I

ONE of the defects in the American system of government, if so superb a confection of the human mind and heart may be said, without indecency, to have any defects at all, lies in the fact that it fails to provide swift and condign punishment for the special crimes of public officials. Even when their wrong-doings take the form of offenses against the ordinary criminal statues of the realm—as, for example, embezzlement, conversion, blackmail, armed entry, kidnaping or common assault—it seems to be very difficult to bring them under the lash of justice; they enjoy, as it were, an unwritten immunity to criminal process, running with the constitutional immunity of United States Senators, who cannot be taken by the *gendarmerie*, even for adultery or bootlegging, while the Senate is in session. The thugs and perjurers of the so-called Department of Justice, during the reign of the Martyr Wilson, committed nearly all the crimes of fraud and violence on the books, and yet, so far as I know, not one of them was ever punished, or, indeed, so much as prosecuted. Several Federal district attorneys, toward the end of that festival of oppression and worse, protested against it publicly, and there were bitter yells from specialists in human liberty and from the relatives, lodge-brothers and creditors of some of the victims, but no Federal grand jury indicted any of the criminals, and no Federal judge condemned them to the hulks. To this day, if my agents are to be believed, the same thing is going on, though perhaps on a more modest scale. Prohibition enforcement officers in all parts of the country are breaking into houses without warrants, destroying property without due process of law, engaging in blackmail in a wholesale manner, and assaulting and murdering citizens almost at their will, and yet one seldom hears of them going to jail for it, and I know of none who has been hanged.

When it comes to crimes that are peculiar to public officials and that arise out of the nature of their legal status, as bigamy and wife-beating arise out of the nature of a married man's, the case is even worse. I allude here to such special offenses as dissipating the public funds, loading the public rolls with useless and pediculous job-holders, letting contracts and franchises to political and private friends, converting public property to private uses, condoning crimes against the government, and administering the laws in a partial and dishonest manner—all of them impossible to the mere citizen and taxpayer, as default in alimony is impossible to the bachelor. Here the ordinary criminal statutes are obviously ineffective, and of special statutes there are almost none. What was the late Mr. Fall guilty of? His accusers, it appears, had to fall back upon the vague charge of conspiracy, which was not unlike accusing a burglar of trespass. With the general run of official delinquents it is impossible to go even so far. Their crimes have no names, and no adequate punishments. Certain high dignitaries, when taken in gross malfeasances, may be impeached, and most lesser ones, though not all, may be cashiered. But neither punishment is harsh enough to be a deterrent, and neither is swift and sure. Since the first days of the Republic but eight Federal job-holders have been brought before the bar of the Senate on impeachment by the House of Representatives, and of these but two have been found guilty and removed from office. Both of the latter were judges; one was convicted of drunkenness on the bench and the other of corrupt dealings with litigants. Is it argued seriously by anyone that, during all those years, but two Federal judges have been guilty of such offenses? Is it argued, indeed, that the bench is wholly guiltless of them, and of all other crimes, today?

Many of the sitting Federal judges, as a matter of fact, are obviously unfit for the duties they have to perform. Some of them owe their jobs to litigants who are habitually before them, and others are admittedly beholden to such corrupt agencies as the Anti-Saloon League. Is it maintained that such dubious fellows make competent and respectable judges, or that the clumsy and enormously costly process of impeachment offers a practicable means of dealing with their frequent and flagrant peccadillos? Plainly not. Even when their obscenities upon the bench become publicly scandalous they are protected by the fact that impeachment is essentially a political, not a judicial process, and that in consequence it is excessively slow and uncertain— in other words, by the fact that it lacks the very characters which legal punishment fundamentally needs. It is, as a matter of practise, almost as safe for a Federal judge to take care of his fellow-golfers and scofflaws as it is for a Prohibition officer to blackmail a bootlegger or for an agent of the Department of Justice to manufacture perjury against so-called Reds. If he belongs to the party in control of Congress he cannot be impeached for any crime short of highway robbery or piracy on the high seas, and even if he belongs to the minority party the citizen who complains of him must be extremely influential to be heard at all, and extremely rich to meet the heavy costs of prosecuting him. In brief, the remedy against him that is offered by the Constitution and the laws is, in substance, no remedy at all. No matter how grossly he violates his oath and the decencies, he commonly remains upon the bench until some grateful litigant or syndicate of litigants offers him a better job.

Moreover, it must be plain that the punishment of impeachment and removal from office, or of removal by executive order, without impeachment, is usually grossly inadequate. When job-holders become so unbearably corrupt or incompetent that they are actually separated from their jobs, they commonly deserve hanging, or, at least, long confinement in the hoosegow. Simply to turn them out, leaving them free to aspire to other offices, is as absurd as it would be to limit a burglar's punishment to kicking him out of the house. The case of the late Denby, Secretary of the Navy, is in point. I have no opinion as to the guilt or innocence of the gentleman; I merely recall the fact that he was accused of the very grave offense of dissipating the national property and imperilling the national defense. It would be difficult to imagine anything more flagrantly anti-social, more thoroughly vicious, more damaging to the common weal; put beside it, such ordinary crimes as arson and larceny seemed relatively harmless. Nevertheless, the worst punishment that could be inflicted upon Denby was the banal one of depriving him of his office. It was impossible, for political reasons, to impeach him or even to attempt to impeach him, and he was simply turned out, with a file of high naval dignitaries saluting him as he left and a great crowd cheering him as he got home. Here cause and effect took on a disproportion that was truly colossal; it was almost as if Czolgosz had been fined $10 for dispatching McKinley. If Denby was innocent, he deserved the salute and the cheers without the loss of his job. And if he was guilty, if only of negligence, he plainly merited at least a geological epoch on Devil's Island.

2

In the effete monarchies of the continent of Europe, now happily abolished by God's will, there was, in the old days of sin, a far more intelligent and effective way of dealing with delinquent officials. Not only were they subject, when taken in downright corruption, to the ordinary processes of the criminal laws; in addition, they were liable to prosecution in special courts for such offenses as were peculiar to their offices. In this business the abominable Prussian state, though founded by Satan, took the lead. It maintained a tribunal in Berlin that devoted itself wholly to the trial of officials accused of malfeasance, corruption, tyranny and incompetence, and any citizen was free to lodge a complaint with the learned judges. The trial was public and in accordance with rules fixed by law. An official found guilty could be punished summarily and in a dozen different ways. He could be reprimanded, reduced in rank, suspended from office for a definite period, transferred to a less desirable job, removed from the rolls altogether, fined, or sent to jail. If he was removed from office he could be deprived of his right to a pension in addition, or fined or jailed in addition. He could be made to pay damages to any citizen he had injured, or to apologize publicly. All this, remember, was in addition to his liability under the ordinary law, and the statutes specifically provided that he could be punished twice for the same offense, once in the ordinary courts and once in the administrative court. Thus, a Prussian official who, imitating the daily routine of the agents of our own Treasury or Department of Justice, assaulted a citizen, invaded his house without a warrant, and seized his property without process of law, could be deprived of his office and fined heavily by the administrative court, sent to jail by an ordinary court, and forced to pay damages to his victim by either or both. Our Federal judges, as a matter of everyday practise, issue thousands of injunctions depriving citizens of their clear right to a jury trial, to the sanctity of domicile and to lawful assemblage, all guaranteed by the Bill of Rights. Had a Prussian judge, overcome by *kaiserliche* passion, undertaken anything of the sort in those far-off days of despotism, any aggrieved citizen might have haled him before the administrative court and recovered heavy damages from him, beside enjoying the felicity of seeing him transferred to some dismal swamp in East Prussia, to listen all day to the unintelligible perjury of Poles. The law specifically provided that responsible officials should be punished, not more leniently than ordinary offenders, but more severely. If a corrupt policeman got six months a corrupt chief of police got two years. More, these statutes were enforced with Prussian barbarity, and the jails were constantly full of errant officials.

I do not propose, of course, that such medieval laws be set up in the United States. We have, indeed, gone far enough in imitating the Prussian system already; if we go much further the moral and enlightened nations of the world will have to unite in a new crusade to put us down. Hints to that effect are not lacking even now; they are heard in England every time the Department of State revives the question of the Bahaman rum trade, and in France every time there is mention of the war debt. As a matter of fact, the Prussian scheme would probably prove ineffective in the Republic, if only because it involved setting up one gang of job-holders to judge and punish another gang. This worked very well in Prussia before the country was civilized by force of arms because, as everyone knows, a Prussian judge was trained in ferocity from infancy, and regarded every man arraigned before him as guilty *ipso facto;* in fact, any thought of a prisoner's possible innocence was abhorrent to him as a reflection upon the *Polizei,* and, hence, by inference, upon the Throne, the whole monarchic idea, and God. But in America, even if they had no other sentiment in common, which would be rarely, judge and prisoner would often be fellow-Democrats or fellow-Republicans, and hence jointly interested in protecting their party against scandal and its members against the loss of their jobs. The operations of the Department of Justice under Mr. Daugherty showed how this community of interest impedes the flow of justice even today; it would be far more obstructive, obviously, if job-holders had to execute the laws against other job-holders, and not merely against the friends of other job-holders. Moreover, the Prussian system has another plain defect: the punishments it provides are, in the main, platitudinous and banal. They lack dramatic quality, and they lack ingenuity and appropriateness. To punish a judge taken in judicial crim. con. by fining him or sending him to jail is a bit too facile and obvious. What is needed is a system (*a*) that does not depend for its execution upon the good-will of job-holders, and (*b*) that provides swift, certain and unpedantic punishments, each fitted neatly to its crime. Such a system, after due prayer, I have devised. It is simple, it is unhackneyed, and I believe that it would work. It is divided into two halves. The first half takes the detection and punishment of the crimes of job-holders away from courts of impeachment, congressional smelling committees, and other such agencies—*i. e.*, away from other job-holders—and vests it in the whole body of free citizens, male and female. The second half provides that any member of that body, having looked into the acts of a job-holder and found him delinquent, may punish him instantly and on the spot, and in any manner that seems appropriate and convenient—and that in case this punishment involves physical damage to the job-holder, the ensuing inquiry by the grand jury or coroner shall confine itself strictly to the question whether the job-holder deserved what he got. In other words, I propose that it shall be no longer *malum in se* for a citizen to pummel, cow-hide, kick, gouge, cut, wound, bruise, maim, burn, club, bastinado, flay or even lynch a job-holder, and that it shall be *malum prohibitum* only to the extent that the punishment exceeds the job-holder's deserts. The amount of this excess, if any, may be determined very conveniently by a petit jury, as other questions

of guilt are now determined.   The flogged judge, or
Congressman, or Prohibition officer, or other job-
holder, on being discharged from hospital—or his
chief heir, in case he has perished—goes before a
grand jury and makes complaint, and, if a true bill
is found, a petit jury is empanelled and all the
evidence is put before it.   If it decides that the job-
holder deserved the punishment inflicted upon him,
the citizen who inflicted it is acquitted with honor.
If, on the contrary, it decides that this punishment
was excessive, then the citizen is adjudged guilty of
assault, mayhem, murder, or whatever it is, in a degree apportioned to the difference between what
the job-holder deserved and what he got, and punishment for that excess follows in the usual course.

3

The advantages of this plan, I believe, are too
patent to need argument.   At one stroke it removes
all the legal impediments which now make the punishment of a recreant job-holder so hopeless a process
and enormously widens the range of possible penalties.   They are now stiff and, in large measure,
illogical; under the system I propose they could be
made to fit the crime precisely.   Say a citizen today
becomes convinced that a certain judge is a jackass—
that his legal learning is defective, his sense of jus-

tice atrophied, and his conduct of cases before him tyrannical and against decency. As things stand, it is entirely impossible to do anything about it. A judge could not be impeached on the mere ground that he is a jackass; the process is far too costly and cumbersome, and there are too many judges liable to the charge. Nor is anything to be gained by denouncing him publicly and urging all good citizens to vote against him when he comes up for re-election, for his term may have ten or fifteen years to run, and even if it expires tomorrow and he is defeated the chances are good that his successor will be quite as bad, and maybe even worse. Moreover, if he is a Federal judge he never comes up for re-election at all; once he has been appointed by the President of the United States, at the advice of his more influential clients and with the consent of their agents in the Senate, he is safe until he is so far gone in senility that he has to be propped on the bench with pillows. But now imagine any citizen free to approach him in open court and pull his nose! Or even, in aggravated cases, to cut off his ears, throw him out of the window, or knock him in the head with an ax! How vastly more attentive he would be to his duties! How diligently he would apply himself to the study of the law! How careful he would be about the rights of litigants before him! How polite and even suave he would become! For judges, like all the rest of us, are vain fellows: they do not enjoy having their noses pulled. Do not forget here that the ignominy resident in the operation would not be abated by the subsequent trial of the puller, even if he should be convicted and jailed. The fact would still be brilliantly remembered that at least one citizen had deemed the judge sufficiently a malefactor to punish him publicly, and to risk going to jail for it. A dozen such episodes, and the career of any judge would be ruined, even though the jails bulged with his critics. He could not maintain his dignity on the bench; even his own catchpolls would snicker at him behind their hands, especially if he showed a cauliflower ear, a black eye or a scar over his bald head. Moreover, soon or late some citizen who had at him would be acquitted by a petit jury, and then, obviously, he would have to retire. It might be provided by law, indeed, that he should be compelled to retire in that case—that an acquittal would automatically vacate the office of the complaining job-holder.

The present system, as I have said, has in late years eloquently demonstrated its ineffectiveness on a colossal scale in the great city of Washington, the seat of the First Chief of the Republic and of a hundred thousand job-holders of gradually lessening puissance, from members of the Cabinet down to janitors, messengers and bookkeepers. All efforts to impeach Daugherty failed; when he was got rid of at last it was by a blow below the belt; in the case of Denby, his fellow-Republicans of Detroit actually treated his dismissal as a martyrdom, and received him when he got home with a band of music and public prayers.   If these eminent men were actually guilty of malfeasance in office they obviously deserved far more rigorous punishment; if they were guilty merely of carelessness and neglect they deserved a severe handling as public nuisances. Under the existing system they got what was virtually no punishment at all; under my system, at the most moderate guess, some bored and impatient citizen, during the long months when they were desperately hanging on to their jobs, would have at least ventured to duck them in the Potomac or set their shirt-tails afire.   I doubt that any jury would have convicted him of excess, even had he held them under while he counted 100,000.   The plain people could not make out just what they had done that was immoral, if anything; but there was an almost universal feeling that they were nuisances, and ought to be got rid of. Even if the citizen who, under my system, had laid hands upon them had been convicted subsequently and sent to jail, the weary newspaper readers of the land would have given three cheers for him, and he would have become a formidable candidate for the presidency on the completion of his term.   Even Dr. Coolidge, I daresay, would have had a very friendly feeling for him, and perhaps might have sent him a box of cigars or some White House pies while he was in jail.

I present my system formally to the consideration of the Congress, and offer to explain it in greater detail before a joint session of both Houses at any time not in conflict with my literary engagements. I am no lawyer, to be sure. I once studied law for a space, but forgot it on closing the books. But I retain enough technic to be convinced that my scheme presents no constitutional difficulties. It violates no constitutional right that I am aware of; on the contrary, it specifically reaffirms the right to a trial by jury, now denied in a wholesale and shameless manner by the Federal courts. It sets up no new corps of corrupt and oppressive enforcement officers; it establishes no new jobs; it does not augment the already excessive powers of the police. If there is any lingering taint of injustice in it, then that injustice would be suffered by job-holders, nine-tenths of whom now rob and persecute the rest of us incessantly, and are fast habilitating the doctrine that we are *feræ naturæ* and have no rights that they are bound to respect. It is a system of criminal law that is democratic in the widest and loftiest sense. It augments the dignity and responsibility of the citizen, and tends to increase his concern with problems of government. It sets higher standards of conduct for public officers than prevail now, and makes corruption and incompetence dangerous. Above all, it breaks down the rigid and unintelligent formalism of our scheme of punishments, and makes it infinitely more pliant, appropriate and various. We have been tending for years to reduce all punishments to two: fine and imprisonment, the first usually no punishment at all, but a mere bribe to escape punishment, and the second often cruel and almost always ineffective. That this tendency is widely regarded as evil is shown by the extra-legal efforts to combat it that are made constantly by the Ku Klux Klan, the American Legion and other such agents of lynch law. My scheme would take over the rich ingenuities of these agents and give them formal legal sanction; it would restore to the art of putting down crime something of the fine bounce and gusto that it had in the Middle Ages, when tort and penalty were united by logical, and even, indeed, æsthetic bonds, and a judge who was imaginative and original was esteemed. The certainty of punishment would daunt the offender, and the uncertainty of its nature would fill him with dread. Once proceeded against, he would become enormously cautious and conscientious. A Congressman with his ears cut off, you may be sure, would not do it again. A judge, after two or three rocket flights through his court-room window, would be forced, by an irresistible psychological process, to give heed thereafter to the Constitution, the statutes, and the common rights of man. Even a police captain or a United States Senator, once floored with a bung-starter or rolled in a barrel, would begin to think.

I dedicate my plan to my country.

XI. ON THE NATURE OF MAN

1

The Animal That Thinks

THAT the great majority of human beings, even under our perfected Christian civilization, are still almost as incapable of rational thought as so many diamond-back terrapin—this is a fact to which we have all been made privy of late by the babbling of eminent psychologists. Granted. But let us not rashly assume that this infirmity is confined strictly to the nether herd—that, above the level where thinking may be said genuinely to begin, it goes on, level by level, to greater and greater heights of clarity and acumen. Nothing, indeed, of the sort. The curve goes upward for a while, but then it begins to flatten, and finally it dips very sharply. Thinking, indeed, is so recent an accomplishment phylogenetically that man is capable of it only in a narrow area, as he is capable of sight and hearing only in narrow areas. To one side lie the instinctive tropisms and intellectual peristaltic motions of the simple, rational only by a sort of pious license; to the other side lie the more complex but even more non-sensical speculations of metaphysicians. The difference between the two is vastly less than is commonly assumed; we are all misled by the sombre, portentous manner of the metaphysicians. The truth is that between a speech by a Salvation Army convert, a Southern Congressman or a Grand Goblin of the Rotary Club and a philosophical treatise by an American Neo-Realist there is no more to choose than between the puling of an infant and the puling of a veteran of the Civil War. Both show the human cerebrum loaded far beyond its Plimsoll mark; both, strictly speaking, are idiotic.

2

Veritas Odium Parit

An old human delusion, largely fostered by theologians, is the one to the effect that truth has a mysterious medicinal power—that its propagation makes the world better and man happier . . . *et cognoscetis veritatem, et veritas liberabit vos.* But is this so-called truth about truth true? It is not. The truth, nine times out of ten, is extremely disturbing and uncomfortable; if it is not grossly discreditable to someone it is apt to be painfully amazing to everyone. The masses of men are thus wise to hold it in suspicion, as they are wise to suspect that other delusion, liberty. Let us turn to an example. The most rational religious ideas held in modern times, at least among Christians, are probably those of the Unitarians; the most nonsensical are those of the Christian Scientists. Yet it must be obvious to every observer that the average Unitarian, even when he is quite healthy, which is not often, is a sour, conscience-striken and unhappy fellow, whereas, the average Christian Scientist, even when he is down with gall-stones, is full of a childish and enviable peace. The one is disquieted by his apprehension of the damning facts about God and the universe; the other is lulled by his magnificent imbecilities. I have had the honor of knowing, in my time, a number of eminent philosophers, some of them intelligent. The happiest among the latter, in his moments of greatest joy, used to entertain himself by drawing up wills leaving his body to a medical college.

3

The Eternal Cripple

Man, at his best, remains a sort of one-lunged animal, never completely rounded and perfect, as a bacillus, say, is perfect. If he shows one valuable quality, it is almost unheard of for him to show any other. Give him a head, and he lacks a heart. Give him a heart of a gallon capacity, and his head holds scarcely a pint. The artist, nine times out of ten, is a dead-beat and given to the debauching of virgins, so-called. The patriot is a bigot, and, more often than not, a cad and a coward. The man of physical bravery is often on a level, intellectually, with a Baptist clergyman. The intellectual giant has bad kidneys and cannot thread a needle. In all my years of search in this world, from the Golden Gate in the West to the Vistula in the East, and from the Orkney Islands in the North to the Spanish Main in the South, I have never met a thoroughly moral man who was honorable.

4

The Test

Don't ask what delusion he entertains regarding God, or what mountebank he follows in politics, or what he springs from, or what he submits to from his wife. Simply ask how he makes his living. It is the safest and surest of all known tests. A man who gets his board and lodging on this ball in an ignominious way is inevitably an ignominious man.

5

National Characters

The character of a nation, like its mind, is always determined, not by the masses of its citizens, but by a small minority of resolute and influential men. Nothing, for example, could be more absurd than the common notion that the French, as a people, are gallant, courageous and fond of hazard. The truth is that they are mainly dull shopkeepers and peace-loving peasants, and have been driven into all their wars of conquest by their masters, who are extraordinarily prehensile and audacious. The French plain people bitterly disapproved the military enterprises of Bonaparte, and resisted his conscriptions by every means within their power. In the late war they abandoned themselves to a melodramatic despair after the first few months, frequently broke and ran under pressure, and were kept in the fight only by heroic devices. The apparent resolution of France was largely external. That is to say, it was supplied by England. Internally, it was confined to a small group of leaders, most of them professional adventurers, and many of them, such as Marshal Foch, of enemy blood. The French masses, despite the enormous military advantages on their side, were ready to quit after every losing battle, and after not a few—for example, the Verdun operations—they did quit.

The character of the Germans, as it was displayed during the war, was also foreign to the great majority of the German people. The Germans are not pugnacious by nature, nor have they any talent for organization; on the contrary, they are incurable particularists, and never meet without quarrelling. Their political history is a history of endless squabbles in the face of the enemy. Fully a half of them believed in Napoleon I at the time he was ravaging their country; in the late war millions of them were deceived by the late Woodrow's hypocritical Fourteen Points—a deliberate and successful device to divide and conquer them. The gigantic skill and resolution visible on the German side during the war were supplied by less than one per cent. of the German people, and so were the harsh, realistic theories which underlaid them. The average German was and is quite incapable of any such theories; they horrify him almost as much as they would horrify a member of the Lake Mohonk Conference. Once the one per cent. of dominating Germans had been disposed of by their heavy losses on the field, the rest of the nation turned out to be a mob of moony sentimentalists, hot for all the democratic fallacies ever heard of, and eager to put down every surviving man of genuine courage and enterprise. That mob will continue to pursue these chimeras until a new race of rulers arises—and then the world will once more mistake the ideas of those rulers for the ideas of the average German.

The English are judged just as inaccurately, and in the same way. There is, for example, the common notion that all Englishmen are good sportsmen, resolute in battle, generous in victory and calm in defeat. It would be difficult to imagine anything more ridiculous. The English masses are probably the worst sportsmen in the world, save only, perhaps, the American masses. During the war their hysterical whoops and yells deafened the universe, and after it was over the so-called khaki election brilliantly displayed the true color of their generosity. To this day, like their brethren of the Republic, they believe it to be quite honorable to pick a German's pocket or rob a German corpse. But there is in England a small minority of men, chiefly Celtic in blood, who practise good sportsmanship as a sort of substitute for religion, and these men are still influential enough to give the hue of their own character to what appears to be the general English character. Once they succumb to democracy, not even American Anglomaniacs will ever mention English sportsmanship again.

6

The Goal

The central aim of civilization, it must be plain, is simply to defy and correct the obvious intent of God, *e. g.*, that five per cent. of the people of Christendom shall die of smallpox every year, that the issue of every love affair shall be a succession of little strangers, that cows shall devote themselves wholly to nursing their calves, that it shall take longer to convey a message from New York to Chicago than it takes to convey one from New York to Newark, that the wicked shall be miserable and the virtuous happy. Has civilization a motto? Then certainly it must be "Not *Thy* will, O Lord, but *ours*, be done!"

7

Psychology at 5 A. M.

It is in the throes of sober second thought, of spiritual *Katzenjammer*, that men reveal their true souls. The Puritan always swears a bloody oath that he will never do it again. The civilized man simply resolves to be a bit more careful next time.

8

The Reward

The cadence at the end is always in the crystalline
and sardonic key of C major. . . The heroic sweat-
ings and strivings of the Knights Templar, for a
whole age the marvel of Christendom, are now embalmed in a single essay by James Anthony Froude,
M.A., LL.D., an historian of charming style but
dubious accuracy. If it were not for that single
essay, it would be difficult, if not impossible, for an
inquirer of English speech to find out what their
finish was, and why they perished from the earth.
Their old stronghold in London is now—what?
An office-building for lawyers, a roost for such rogues
as they would have put to the sword at sight. And
Palestine, for which they died by the thousand, is
now given over to *Schnorrer* and *Meshulachim* from
Grand street and the Mile End road.

9

The Altruist

A large part of altruism, even when it is perfectly honest, is grounded upon the fact that it is

uncomfortable to have unhappy people about one. This is especially true in family life.   A man makes sacrifices to his wife's desires, not because he greatly enjoys giving up what he wants himself, but because he would enjoy it even less to see her cutting a sour face across the dinner table.

10

The Man of Honor

The difference between a moral man and a man of honor is that the latter regrets a discreditable act, even when it has worked and he has not been caught.

XII. BUGABOO

ALL of the Great Thinkers of the world, East, West, North and South, have been alarming their customers, for two or three years past, with the same bugaboo. According to the New York *Times* and the Department of State, there must be a complete restoration of the capitalistic system in Russia and Mexico, or our sweet Christian civilization will go to pot. According to the masterminds of France, the Germans must first lose all their trade and then pay 10,000 cents on the dollar, or our sweet Christian civilization will go to pot. According to H. G. Wells, the Treaty of Versailles must be denounced by all parties to it, or our sweet Christian civilization will go to pot. And so on, and so on. On the main point the propagandists of all schools are unanimously agreed: that the civilization of the West teeters on the edge of an abyss, and that a few more wobbles will send it over. The barbarians once more thunder upon the gates of Rome. Let the turmoils within go on for a brief while longer, and they will burst in with their hellish cries, and every great boon and usufruct that men

have sweated and died for since the days of Charle-
magne, from the cathedral at Rheims to the pneu-
matic automobile tire, and from fiddle music to
diphtheria antitoxin, and from the inferiority complex to the bichloride tablet, will vanish in one
universal catastrophe. Blood drips from the moon;
another general war impends. This war, according
to Will H. Irwin, a soothsayer employed by the
Saturday Evening Post, will be so colossal a butchery
that there will be no survivors save a few undertakers
and profiteers, and no material salvage save a few
stone quarries and a couple of million bales of
worthless bonds.

Personally, I should be glad to see such a war,
for it seems to me that the human race has run on
long enough—that the high gods would show unac-
customed sense if they dropped it into hell and so
ended the farce. I know of no existing nation that
deserves to live, and I know of very few individuals.
But despite the fact that my wishes are thus on the
side of Dr. Irwin's thought, I find it quite impossible
to follow him. In brief, I see absolutely no sign
of a general *débâcle.* On the contrary, it seems to
me that the thing we call civilization was never
more secure than it is today, either in Europe or in
America. More bloodshed, of course, is pretty
certain to come; the French, to name only one people,

are obviously headed for another shambles. But
that is a small matter, almost a private matter.
Even the complete destruction of France would not
materially damage civilization, save, perhaps, in
the eyes of touring American Puritans, a-search for
a moral oasis. I also incline to think that England and the United States will be by the ears before
many years have come and gone, and that one or
the other of them, probably the United States, will
get a severe beating. But they have fought before, and civilization was scarcely aware of it.
Either could be wiped out utterly, and it would still
be possible to buy Ford parts, Bibles, oil stocks,
canned salmon, union suits, First Folio Shakespeares,
hair tonics, books on sex hygiene, diamonds, coffins,
dice, dog soap, glass eyes, and all the other great
blessings of our Christian *Kultur*. Both could be
destroyed, wholly and horribly, and men in Italy
would continue to grow excellent wine, and men in
Germany would continue to pursue the colloids and
the cocci, and men in Scandinavia would continue to
shiver and curse God through their long, grisly
Winter nights, and so keep the world supplied with
its normal doses of theology, metaphysics and political theory. Moreover, there are the Chinese. If
the entire population of Christendom were disposed
of by some cosmic delousing operation the Chinese

would have a chance—a chance denied to them to-day, in free competition, by their superior dignity, decency and sense of honor.

The interdependence of nations, indeed, is much overestimated by sentimentalists, chiefly of the economic faculty. They permit the gyrations of foreign exchange to alarm them. But what is it to a man in Kansas, or Uruguay, or Saskatchewan, expressed in hard figures, that a million Poles have been slaughtered, or that the Turks have again ravaged Armenia, or that the British and Dutch are at odds over human liberty and the oil-wells of Mesopotamia, or that Belgrade has fallen, or that the French refuse to go back to work but propose to live hereafter by highway robbery? It is, at most, a matter of ten per cent. This is all he feels, and this is all he cares. If he shows any excitement or even any interest it is because some drive manager has played upon his credulities, as Dr. Wells seeks to play upon the credulities of all of us. For one, I refuse to be alarmed. If Paris were burned tomor-row, I'd scarcely know it on my estates in Maryland, feeding upon my razor-back hams, listening to Caruso's ghost, and reading the state papers of Thomas Jefferson. Even if I tired of that idyllic life and went abroad, I'd admire the ruins quite as much as I have ever admired the Trocadero or the Eiffel tower. Both, perhaps, would escape the fire—and no doubt the incendiaries would make off with the best things in the Luxembourg and the Louvre. Nor am I greatly alarmed by the current doctrine that the late war stamped out the best strains of all the contesting nations, and that they are rapidly sinking to the level of their lower classes. This alarm is raised in an inflammatory book called "Is America Safe for Democracy?" by one William McDougall, a Scotchman imported to civilize the sophomores at Harvard. The McDougall also raises and parades another hobgoblin, once a favorite of the immortal zany, Major-General Roosevelt. That is the bugaboo of race suicide, especially among the upper classes. The wops in the ditch and the Slovaks in the mining towns, it appears, breed up to the limit of human endurance, but bank presidents seldom have more than four or five legitimate children, and the great majority of poets, metaphysicians, Oxford dons, lady Ph.D.s, assyriologists and moving-picture actors are childless, and perhaps even sterile. At the present rate of reproduction, says Prof. McDougall, 1000 Harvard graduates of today will have but 50 descendants 200 years hence, whereas 1000 Rumanians will have 100,000.

But what of it? On the one hand this gay professor assumes far too readily that Harvard graduates, taking one with another, deserve to be ranked as first-rate men, and on the other hand he greatly overestimates the number of first-rate men needed to run the world, and to insure a reasonable rate of human progress. The fact is that the safeguarding and development of civilization are and always have been in the exclusive care of a very small minority of human beings of each generation, and that the rest of the human race consists wholly of deadheads. Consider, for example, the telephone, a very characteristic agent of Christian advancement. It has been invented, perfected, organized and brought to every door in our own time by less than 20 men—nay, by less than 10 men. All the others who have made it, financed and installed it have been simply trailers. All the rest of the human race has taken a free ride. The number of such first-rate men in the world is always overestimated, and it is fatuously assumed that they are identical with the wealthier minority of the population. Prof. Dr. McDougall himself falls into this last error. He proves—what everyone knew already—that the children of well-to-do parents are brighter, by pedagogical standards, than the children of poor folk, but this fact is of no significance. If it were, then pedagogues themselves would rank as first-rate men, which is an absurdity; they are, in fact, generally stupid, and seldom produce anything of value to the world. The test of a first-rate man is not to be made by the criteria of schoolmarms. It is to be made by asking the

simple question: Has he ever said or done anything
that was not said or done before, and is it something
of positive and permanent value to the human race?
If the answer is yes, then he belongs to the superior
minority; if it is no, then he belongs to the mob, no
matter how brilliantly he may pass examinations, and
no matter how greatly he may prosper under the civilization that his superiors have fostered and
developed.

The number of men who can pass this test is always extremely small—vastly smaller than the un-
critical worshipers of politicians, university presidents, prima donna theologians, opera singers, lawyers, popular philosophers, successful authors and
other such human Fords usually assume. How
many exist at the present moment in the United
States? I turn to "Who's Who in America" and find
23,443 names. But a brief inspection is sufficient
to show that only a small minority are borne by first-
rate men. I run over page after page and find nothing but Fords—an army general who has done absolutely nothing save obey orders and draw his pay,
three authors of the eighth rate, five or six pedagogues, a theologian or two, a Federal judge—who
ever heard of a Federal judge who left the world
more intelligent, more virtuous or more efficient than
he found it?—a publisher of bad books, two Con-
gressmen, a bishop. I begin to despair. Finally,

I find a first-rate man: Bush of the Bush Terminals.
One in 35.   The proportion, I think, is fair for the
whole book.   This makes 670 first-rate Americans in
our time.   Call it 700 to be safe.   But race-suicide
among the upper classes will make it impossible to
produce even the 700 in the next generation?   Nonsense!   It is not necessary that *every* first-rate man
leave children behind him; it is only necessary that
a few of them in each generation do so.   Nature will
do the rest.   The first-rate character may be concealed for a generation or two, but soon or late it will
reveal itself, and sometimes in many individuals.
This explains the common notion that first-rate men
are often produced in low life, *e. g.*, the case of Lincoln.   They are, but not by low-lifers.   Here the
devil helps the angels, and the sinfulness of man
takes on a high human utility.   Often the cross is
concealed in forgotten generations.   The good blood
is apparently lost in the flood of proletarian bilge—
but suddenly it begins to run red and clear, and the
platitudinarians have another up-from-slavery chap-
ter to wag their ears over.   I believe fully that the
first-rate men of the world constitute a distinct and
separate species—that they have little, if anything,
in common with the lower orders of men.   But the
two races, fortunately for human progress, are mu-
tually fertile.   If they ever cease to be, then God
help us all!   But there is absolutely no sign that they

are ceasing to be. So long as they remain as they
are there need be no worry about the future of civilization. The danger is that first-rate men may grow
too numerous, and so arouse the hatred of the lower
orders, as happened in Greece. The United States
now accommodates 700. If the number rose to
1000 I fear that the churches, the newspapers, Congress and the American Legion would grow restless,
and that the catastrophe dreamed of by Prof. McDougall would begin to cast its shadows before.

Meanwhile, all the current pulling of long faces
is absurd. There is not the slightest sign that the
basic elements of modern civilization, such as it is,
are in any danger, proximately or remotely. Europe, at the moment, is a bit weary, but no actual barbarians are thundering at the gate; all the recognizable barbarians, in fact, are retreating sadly into
their native jungles, with troubles of their own.
There is no decline in Christian *morale;* if anything,
there is far too much Christian *morale* on tap. The
one thing that one may say accurately is that there
is a struggle for control within the borders of civilization itself, to wit, between the masses of simple and
stupid men and various minorities of extremely
egoistic and determined men. But neither side is
trying to destroy civilization, save in the indignant
visions of the other. On the contrary, both are trying their best to preserve it, and whether one side

wins or the other it will be duly preserved. Ten years hence it will be just as easy to send a picture postcard or to be beaten by a policeman as it is today, and wherever one may buy a picture postcard the arts are safe and wherever one may be beaten by a policeman law and order are safe, and when the arts and law and order are safe, then civilization is also safe. False analogies are at the bottom of most of the current fears—that is, when they are honest. The analogy with Rome, so often cited, is especially nonsensical. A few hundred thousand Romans were surrounded by countless millions of barbarians, and the barbarians had arms quite as good as those of the Romans. Where is any similar horde to be found today? Are the Japs dangerous? Plainly not, save perhaps to the United States. The Japs, with all of the odds on their side, took more than two years to beat the Russians; they would stand up before a European coalition no more than 10 days. The Chinese? They don't want Europe; they want only China. The blacks of Africa? Two German divisions could dispose of all of them, given a fair, stand-up battle, in two hours. Nor is any genuine fear to be deduced from the fate of the late Confederacy in America. The intellectual collapse of the Southern States after the Civil War was purely a local and geographical matter. Most of the surviving Southerners who had been civilized before the war simply moved North, leaving only a few cripples, the darkeys and a mob of poor white trash behind. But civilization in the United States was certainly not affected; in fact, the mixing of Southerners and Northerners in the North probably improved it. Today, a half century afterward, even some of the Southern poor whites are becoming relatively civilized. A book store has been opened in New Orleans, a man in Mobile has bought a violoncello, and only the other day, in Georgia, a white man was actually taken by the constabulary for killing a dozen Negroes.

What the authors of elegies mistake for the collapse of civilization is simply the internal struggle that I have mentioned—the ages-old combat between the haves and the have-nots, now rendered transiently acute by a parlous shortening of the things fought for. The ultimate issue of that struggle seems to me to be plain enough. The have-nots will be given a drubbing, and under the protection of a new and unprecedentedly vigorous and daring capitalism the thing called Christian civilization will be promoted as it has never been promoted before. My arteries harden so fast—a consequence of my constant and quixotic sacrifice of myself to the common weal— that I cannot hope to live into the full flush of that new Golden Age, but I can at least smack my lips over it in anticipation. What I see is a vast horde of inferior men broken, after a hopeless, fruitless fight, to the hard, uninspiring labor of the world— a race of slaves superbly regimented, and kept steadily in order by great brigades of propagandists, official optimists, scare-mongers, Great Thinkers and rev. clergy.   And over them a minority of capitalist overlords, well-fed, well-protected, highly respected, politely envied, and lavishly supplied with endless stores of picture postcards, gasoline, silk underwear, mayonnaise, Pontet Canet, toilet soap and phonograph records.

The battle, in fact, is already half won.   In France and the United States capitalism can weather any conceivable storm.   In England it craftily encourages labor to a combat that will be to a finish, and with capital on top.   In Italy it is already in the saddle.   In Germany only the Junkers stave off the inevitable victory of money.   In Russia the Bolsheviks help capital everywhere by reducing the cause of the have-nots to an absurdity.   The other countries are not dogs, but mere tails. . . . The United States, I believe, will see the thing brought to its finest flower.   There were no war losses here, but only profits.   In all other countries, the conscripts of the war are restless, and inclined to move toward the Left.   Here they are already superbly organized to serve capital, and give the final touch of felicity to the situation by serving it for nothing.

On the evening of the same day that an American Legionary has his wages reduced 40 per cent. and his hours of labor increased 25 per cent., he goes out at his own risk and expense and helps to tar and feather some visionary who tries to convince him that he has been swindled. Meanwhile, the Supreme Court of New York decides formally that "the courts . . . must stand at all times as the representatives of capital," and the newspapers commend the dictum in lavish terms. . . . I sing Utopia. It is about to burst upon us.

XIII. ON GOVERNMENT

1

"GOVERNMENT," said William Godwin in that "Enquiry Concerning Political Justice" which got Shelley two wives and lost him £6000 a year, "can have no more than two legitimate purposes: the suppression of injustice against individuals within the community, and the common defense against external invasion." The dictum, after a hundred and thirty-one years, remains unimproved and perhaps unimprovable. Today, to be sure, with Darwin behind us, we'd make some change in its terms: what Godwin was trying to say, obviously, was that the central aim of government was to ameliorate the struggle for existence—to cherish and protect the dignity of man in the midst of the brutal strife of *Homo neanderthalensis*. But that change would be simply substituting a *cliché* of the Nineteenth Century for one of the Eighteenth. All the furious discussion of the subject that has gone on in the intervening time has not changed the basic idea in the slightest. To the plain man of today, as to the most fanatical Liberal or Socialist, government appears primarily as a device for compensating his weakness, a machine for protecting him in rights that he could not make secure with his own arm. Even the Tory holds the same view of it: its essential function, to him, is to safeguard his property against the lascivious desires of those who, if they were not policed, would be tempted to grab it. "Government," said George Washington, "is not reason, it is not eloquence—it is force." Bad government is that which is weak, irresolute and lacking in constabulary enterprise; when one has defined it, one has also defined a bad bishop, cavalry captain or policeman. Good government is that which delivers the citizen from the risk of being done out of his life and property too arbitrarily and violently—one that relieves him sufficiently from the barbaric business of guarding them to enable him to engage in gentler, more dignified and more agreeable undertakings, to his own content and profit, and the advantage, it may be, of the commonwealth.

Unfortunately, this function is performed only imperfectly by any of the forms of government now visible in Christendom, and Dr. Johnson was perhaps justified in dismissing them all as but various aspects of the same fraud. The citizen of today, even in the most civilized states, is not only secured but defectively against other citizens who aspire to exploit and injure him—for example, highwaymen, bankers, quack doctors, clergymen, sellers of oil stock and contaminated liquor, and so-called reformers of all sorts,—and against external foes, military, commercial and philosophical; he is also exploited and injured almost without measure by the government itself—in other words, by the very agency which professes to protect him. That agency becomes, indeed, one of the most dangerous and insatiable of the inimical forces present in his everyday environment. He finds it more difficult and costly to survive in the face of it than it is to survive in the face of any other enemy. He may, if he has prudence, guard himself effectively against all the known varieties of private criminals, from stockbrokers to pickpockets and from lawyers to kidnapers, and he may, if he has been burnt enough, learn to guard himself also against the rogues who seek to rob him by the subtler device of playing upon his sentimentalities and superstitions: charity mongers, idealists, soul-savers, and others after their kind. But he can no more escape the tax-gatherer and the policemen, in all their protean and multitudinous guises, than he can escape the ultimate mortician. They beset him constantly, day in and day out, in ever-increasing numbers and in ever more disarming masks and attitudes. They invade his liberty, affront his dignity and greatly incommode his search for happiness, and every year

they demand and wrest from him a larger and larger
share of his worldly goods. The average American
of today works more than a day in every week
to support his government. It already costs him
more than his pleasures and most as much as his
vices, and in another half century, no doubt, it will
begin to cost as much as his necessities.

These gross extortions and tyrannies, of course,
are all practised on the theory that they are not only
unavoidable, but also laudable—that government op-
presses its victims in order to confer upon them the
great boons mentioned by Godwin. But that theory,
I believe, begins to be quite as dishonest as the chiro-
practor's pretense that he pummels his patient's spine
in order to cure his cancer: the actual object, obviously, is simply to cure his solvency. What keeps
such notions in full credit, and safeguards them
against destructive analysis, is chiefly the survival
into our enlightened age of a concept hatched in the
black days of absolutism—the concept, to wit, that
government is something that is superior to and quite
distinct from all other human institutions—that it
is, in its essence, not a mere organization of ordinary
men, like the Ku Klux Klan, the United States Steel
Corporation or Columbia University, but a tran-
scendental organism composed of aloof and impersonal powers, devoid wholly of self-interest and
not to be measured by merely human standards.

One hears it spoken of, not uncommonly, as one hears the law of gravitation and the grace of God spoken of—as if its acts had no human motive in them and stood clearly above human fallibility. This concept, I need not argue, is full of error. The government at Washington is no more impersonal than the cloak and suit business is impersonal. It is operated by precisely the same sort of men, and to almost the same ends. When we say that it has decided to do this or that, that it proposes or aspires to do this or that—usually to the great cost and inconvenience of nine-tenths of us—we simply say that a definite man or group of men has decided to do it, or proposes or aspires to do it; and when we examine this group of men realistically we almost invariably find that it is composed of individuals who are not only not superior to the general, but plainly and depressingly inferior, both in common sense and in common decency—that the act of government we are called upon to ratify and submit to is, in its essence, no more than an act of self-interest by men who, if no mythical authority stood behind them, would have a hard time of it surviving in the struggle for existence.

2

These men, in point of fact, are seldom if ever moved by anything rationally describable as public spirit; there is actually no more public spirit among them than among so many burglars or street-walkers. Their purpose, first, last and all the time, is to promote their private advantage, and to that end, and *that* end alone, they exercise all the vast powers that are in their hands. Sometimes the thing they want is mere security in their jobs; sometimes they want gaudier and more lucrative jobs; sometimes they are content with their jobs and their pay but yearn for more power. Whatever it is they seek, whether security, greater ease, more money or more power, it has to come out of the common stock, and so it diminishes the shares of all other men. Putting a new job-holder to work decreases the wages of every wage-earner in the land—not enough to be noticed, perhaps, but enough to leave its mark. Giving a job-holder more power takes something away from the liberty of all of us: we are less free than we were in proportion as he has more authority. Theoretically, we get something for what we thus give up, but actually we usually get absolutely nothing. Suppose two-thirds of the members of the national House of Representatives were dumped into the Washington garbage incinerator tomorrow, what would we lose to offset our gain of their salaries and the salaries of their parasites? It may be plausibly argued, of course, that the House itself is necessary to our happiness and salvation—that we need it as we need trolley conductors, chiropodists and the men who bite off puppies' tails. But even if that be granted—and I, for one, am by no means disposed to grant it— the plain fact remains that all the useful work the House does might be done just as well by fifty men, and that the rest are of no more utility to the commonwealth, in any rational sense, than so many tightrope walkers or teachers of mah jong.

The Fathers, when they launched the Republic, were under no illusions as to the nature of government. Washington's view of its inner nature I have already quoted; Jefferson it was who said sagely that "that government is best which governs least." The Constitution in its first form, perhaps, was designed chiefly to check the rising pretensions of the lower orders, drunk with the democratic fustian of the Revolutionary era, but when the Bill of Rights was added to it its guns began to point more especially at the government itself, *i. e.*, at the class of job-holders, ever bent upon oppressing the citizen to the limit of his endurance. It is, perhaps, a fact provocative of sour mirth that the Bill of Rights was designed trustfully to prohibit forever two of the favorite crimes of all known governments: the seizure of private property without adequate compensation and the invasion of the citizen's liberty without justifiable cause and due process of law. It is a fact provocative of mirth yet more sour that the execution of these prohibitions was put into the hands of courts, which is to say, into the hands of lawyers, which is to say, into the hands of men specifically educated to discover legal excuses for dishonest, dishonorable and anti-social acts. The actual history of the Constitution, as everyone knows, has been a history of the gradual abandonment of all such impediments to governmental tyranny. Today we live frankly under a government of men, not of laws. What is the Bill of Rights to a Roosevelt, a Wilson, a Palmer, a Daugherty, a Burns? Under such tin-horn Cæsars the essential enmity between government and citizen becomes only too plain, and one gets all the proof that is needed of the eternal impossibility of protecting the latter against the former. The government can not only evoke fear in its victims; it can also evoke a sort of superstitious reverence. It is thus both an army and a church, and with sharp weapons in both hands it is virtually irresistible. Its personnel, true enough, may be changed, and so may the external forms of the fraud it practises, but its inner nature is immutable.

Politics, as hopeful men practise it in the world, consists mainly of the delusion that a change in form is a change in substance. The American colonists, when they got rid of the Potsdam tyrant, believed fondly that they were getting rid of oppressive taxes forever and setting up complete liberty. They found almost instantly that taxes were higher than ever, and before many years they were writhing under the Alien and Sedition Acts. The French, when they threw off the monarchy at last, looked forward to a Golden Age of peace, plenty and freedom. They are now wrecked by war, bankrupted beyond any chance of recovery, and hag-ridden by an apparently unbreakable combination of the most corrupt and cynical politicians ever seen in the world. The experience of the Russians and Germans is even more eloquent. The former have been ruined by their saviors, and in so far as they have any power of reflection left, long for the restoration of the tyranny they once ascribed to the devil. The latter, delivered from the Hohenzollerns, now find the Schmidts and Krauses ten times as expensive and oppressive. Six months after the republic was set up a German cabinet minister, for the first time in the history of the nation, was in flight over the border, his loot under his arm. In the first flush of surprise and indignation the people took to assassinating politicians, but before long they gave it up as hopeless: Schmidt fell but Kraus still lived, and so government kept its vitality and its character. Many Germans, reduced to despair, now advocate a complete abolition of political government; if Stinnes had lived they would have tried to make him dictator of the country. But political government, *i. e.,* government by professional job-holders, would have remained in fact, despite its theoretical abolition, and its nature would have been unchanged.

If downright revolution is thus incapable of curing the disease, the ordinary reforms that men believe in sink to the level of bald quackeries. Consider, for example, the history of so-called Civil Service Reform in the United States. It came in on a wave of intense public indignation against the whole governmental imposture; it represented a violent and romantic effort to substitute an ideal of public service for the familiar harsh reality of public exploitation. For fifty years the American people had sweated and suffered under the spoils system, that lovely legacy of the "reforms" of the Jackson era. By the opening of the eighties they were ready to dispose of it by fair means or foul. The job-holder, once theoretically a freeman discharging a lofty and necessary duty, was seen clearly to be no more than a rat devouring the communal corn; his public position was indistinguishable from that of a child-stealer, a well-poisoner or a Sunday-school superintendent; and that of his brother, the government contractor and purveyor, was even lower. Many men of both classes, including some very important ones, were clapped into jail, and many others had to depart for Canada between days, along with the nightly squad of clerical seducers and absconding bank cashiers. Thereupon seers and prophets arose to lead the people out of the wilderness. A few wild ones proposed, in effect, that government be abolished altogether, but the notion outraged democratic sentiment, and so most of them followed the job-holders into jail; some, in fact, were put to death by more or less due process of law. The majority of soothsayers were less revolutionary: they proposed only that the race of job-holders be reformed by force, that government be purged and denaturized.

This was undertaken by what came to be called Civil Service Reform. The essence of Civil Service Reform was the notion that the job-holder, in return for his high prerogatives and immunities, should be compelled to do an honest day's work—that he should fit himself for it by hard effort, as a barber fits himself for cutting hair. Led by such men of Vision as E. L. Godkin, Charles J. Bonaparte and Theodore Roosevelt (that, of course, was before Roosevelt deserted the flag and became himself the archetypical job-holder), the reformers proceeded grimly toward the dreadful purpose of making the job-holder a mere slave, like a bookkeeper in a whole-sale house. His pay and emoluments were cut down and his labors were increased. Once the proudest and most envied citizen of the Republic, free to oppress all other citizens to the limit of their endurance, he became at one stroke a serf groaning in a pen, with a pistol pointed at his head. If, despite the bars and artillery surrounding him, his thrift enabled him to make a show of decent prosperity, he was clapped into prison *ipso facto,* and almost without a trial. A few short years saw his fall from the dizziest height of ease to the lowest abyss of misery.

This, of course, could not go on, else politics would have tumbled into chaos and government would have lost its basic character; nay, its very life. What is more, it did *not* go on, for human ingenuity, despite the troubles of the time, was still functioning, and presently it found a remedy for the disease—a remedy so perfect, indeed, that the patient did not know he was taking it. That remedy was achieved by the simple process of making two slight changes in the ideal of Civil Service Reform itself. First the word Reform was lopped off, and then the word Civil. There remained, then, only Service. This Service saved the day for the job-holder; it gave him a new lease upon his job; it diverted public suspicion from him; it converted him from a criminal into a sort of philanthropist. It remains with us today, the heir and assign of the old spoils system, as the bootlegger is the heir and assign of the saloon-keeper.

3

The chief achievement of Service is that it has sucked reform into the governmental orbit, and so made it official and impeccable—more, highly profitable. The old-time reformer was one who got nothing for his psychic corn-cures and shin-plasters —who gave them away freely to all comers, seeking only righteousness himself—who often, indeed, took a beating into the bargain. The new reformer, safe in a government job, with a drastic and complex law behind him, is one who is paid in legal tender, unfailingly proffered, for his passionate but usually unintelligible services to humanity—a prophet of the new enlightenment, a priest at a glittering and immense shrine. He is the fellow who enforces the Volstead Act, the Mann Act, all the endless laws for putting down sin. He is the bright evangelist who tours the country teaching mothers how to have babies, spreading the latest inventions in pedagogy, road-making, the export trade, hog-raising and vegetable-canning, waging an eternal war upon illiteracy, hookworm, the white slave trade, patent medicines, the foot and mouth disease, cholera infantum, adultery, rum. He is, quite as often as not, female; he is a lady Ph.D., cocksure, bellicose, very well paid. Male or female, he represents the new governmental tyranny; he is Vision, vice the spoils system, retired. The old-time job-holder, penned in the cage of the Civil Service, is now only a peon, a brother to the ox. He has to work quite as hard as if he labored for Judge Gary or Henry Ford, and he is very much worse paid. The high prerogatives and usufructs of government have slipped out of his hands. They are exercised and enjoyed today by the apostles of Service, a horde growing daily, vastly and irresistibly, in numbers, impudence, power and pay.

Few of the groaning taxpayers of These States, indeed, realize how far this public merchandizing of buncombe has displaced the old spoils system, or how much it is costing them every year. During the Civil War an army contractor who went to Washington looking for loot announced frankly what he was after; as a result, he was constantly under suspicion, and was lucky if he got away with as much as $100,000; only a few Vanderbilts and Morgans actually stole more. During the late war he called himself a dollar-a-year-man, put on a major's uniform, took oath to die if need be for the cause of democracy—and went home with a million, at least. The job-holder has undergone a similar metamorphosis; maybe apotheosis would be a better aimed word. In the days of the spoils system he was, at best, an amateurish and inept performer. The only reason he ever offered for demanding a place at the public trough was that he deserved it—that he had done his share to elect the ticket. The easy answer to him was that he was an obvious loafer and scoundrel, and deserved nothing. But what answer is to

be made to his heir and assign, the evangelist of
Service, the prophet of Vision? He doesn't start
off with a bald demand for a job; he starts off with
a Message. He has discovered the long-sought sure
cure for all the sorrows of the world; he has the in-
fallible scheme for putting down injustice, misery,
ignorance, suffering, sin; his appeal is not to the
rules of a sinister and discreditable game, but to the
bursting heart of humanity, the noblest and loftiest
sentiments of man. His job is never in the fore-
ground; it is concealed in his Vision. To get at the
former one must first dispose of the latter. Well,
who is to do it? What true-born American will
volunteer for the cynical office? Half are too
idiotic and the rest are too cowardly. It takes
courage to flaunt and make a mock of Vision—and
where is courage?

Certainly not in this imperial commonwealth of
natural kneebenders and marchers in parades. Nowhere else in Christendom, save only in France, is
government more extravagant, nonsensical, unintelligent and corrupt than here, and nowhere else is it
so secure. It becomes a sort of crime even to protest against its villainies; all the late investigations
of waste and corruption in Washington were attacked
and brought to wreck in the name of duty, decorum,
patriotism. The citizen objecting to felony by the
agents of the sovereign state, acting in its name,

found himself posted as an anarchist! There was, of course, some logic in this imbecility, as there is in everything insane. It was felt that too violent an onslaught upon the disease might do gross damage to the patient, that the attempt to extirpate what was foul and excrescent might imperil what was useful and necessary. Is government, then, useful and necessary? So is a doctor. But suppose the dear fellow claimed the right, every time he was called in to prescribe for a bellyache or a ringing in the ears, to raid the family silver, use the family tooth-brushes, and execute the *droit de seigneur* upon the house-maid? Is it simply a coincidence that the only necessary functionaries who actually perform any comparable brigandage are the lawyers—the very men who, under democracy, chiefly determined the form, policies and acts of the government?

This great pox of civilization, alas, I believe to be incurable, and so I propose no new quackery for its treatment. I am against dosing it, and I am against killing it. All I presume to argue is that something would be accomplished by viewing it more realistically—by ceasing to let its necessary and perhaps useful functions blind us to its ever-increasing crimes against the ordinary rights of the free citizen and the common decencies of the world. The fact that it is generally respected—that it possesses effective machinery for propagating and safeguarding that

respect—is the main shield of the rogues and vaga-
bonds who use it to exploit the great masses of
diligent and credulous men. Whenever you hear
anyone bawling for more respect for the laws,
whether it be a Coolidge on his imperial throne or an
humble county judge in his hedge court, you have
before you one who is trying to use them to his private advantage; whenever you hear of new legislation
for putting down dissent and rebellion you may be
sure that it is promoted by scoundrels. The extortions and oppressions of government will go on
so long as such bare fraudulence deceives and dis-
arms the victims—so long as they are ready to
swallow the immemorial official theory that protesting
against the stealings of the archbishop's secretary's
nephew's mistress' illegitimate son is a sin against
the Holy Ghost. They will come to an end when
the victims begin to differentiate clearly between
government as a necessary device for maintaining
order in the world and government as a device for
maintaining the authority and prosperity of pred-
atory rascals and swindlers. In other words, they
will come to an end on the Tuesday following the
first Monday of November preceding the Resurrec-
tion Morn.

XIV. TOWARD A REALISTIC ÆSTHETIC

1

The Nature of Art

THE dominating purpose of man in the world is to conquer Nature, which is to say, to defeat the plain intent of God. God and man are the eternal antagonists. Man makes progress every time he wins a new victory; if he can hold his gains his progress is real. Poetry is one device for defeating God. Its aim is to escape some of the pains of reality by denying boldly that they exist—by saying, in some form or other, that "I am the captain of my soul" and "all's well with the world." This denial gives some comfort to human hearts, particularly to the more romantic sort; it is a poor substitute, perhaps, for the actual conquest of the harsh facts, but it is nevertheless a substitute. Religion operates in precisely the same way; its primary purpose is to read an intelligible and even laudable motive into the inscrutable assaults of God. Poetry, of course, is a cut higher than religion, logically speaking. It denies the facts, but it denies them more or less speciously and sometimes almost convincingly; it seldom, if ever, has to enounce the thumping and obvious absurdities that religion relies upon. But it is nevertheless a denial of reality, and hence very deficient as an agent of progress. Science is far more effective. It does not deny the imbecilities and horrors of Nature; it sets about actually modifying them, and even abolishing them. When science conquers it is usually a conquest that is permanent. We have got rid of wolves, ghosts and yellow fever finally and almost completely; they no longer bother civilized men. In the same way we have got rid of some of the horrors that religion raised—horrors worse than those it sought to lay. Science is not only effective against Nature; it is also effective against the dangerous remedies formerly employed against Nature.

Religion and the arts are thus only second-rate means of achieving man's chief purpose in the world. They give him a lot of comfort, but they expose him to the dangers which always follow the denial of reality. The man who believes that God is personally interested in him and will save him from harm is in a far more perilous situation than the man who knows better; so, also, with the man who believes that what poetry says is true. The other arts, having less ideational content, are a good deal less menacing. The statements that architecture makes, for example, are not against the plain facts but in accord with the plain facts—for example, that St. Thomas' Church is more beautiful than the Jersey marshes or its own rector. So with music, and, to some extent, with painting, though painting is hampered by its function of representing Nature— that is, of reproducing Nature without comment, or with very feeble and ineffective comment. Painting will become a genuinely valuable art when it finally abandons representation. The portrait of an ugly woman, even though the artist tries to ameliorate her ugliness a bit, remains almost as horrible as the ugly woman herself. That is to say, the artist simply multiplies and reinforces the horror already concocted by God.

The arts that avoid representation are like science in this: that they actually improve upon Nature, and so add permanently to man's comfort and happiness in the world. The Parthenon is not a mere idle denial of the facts of life, like poetry; it is a positive improvement upon the facts of life; it makes a Greek hilltop appreciably more beautiful than it was as God made it, and so mitigates the horror of life to man. Music achieves the same thing, and even more effectively. The nine Beethoven symphonies do not deny any palpable fact; they merely create new facts that are more agreeable than those previously existing. There are no sounds in Nature comparable to the lovely sounds that Beethoven evokes. Here man shows himself definitely the superior of God. Poetry, of course, also achieves a measure of genuine and permanent beauty. But it can do so only in its character as a form of music. The blank verse of Shakespeare, as music, is as noble a creation as the symphonies of Beethoven. But all poetry, even the best, is corrupted by its logical content. It almost invariably *says* something, and that something is almost always untrue. When man speaks or believes an untruth he certainly makes no progress with his conquest of Nature. On the contrary, he plainly gives up the battle, at least for the moment. Instead of fighting resolutely and effectively, and so improving his state, he simply buries his head in the sand.

2

The One-Legged Art

To me, at all events, painting seems to be half an alien among the fine arts. Its credentials, of course, are sounder than those of acting, but they are surely not as sound as those of music, poetry, drama, sculpture and architecture. The trouble with painting is that it lacks movement, which is to say, the

chief function of life. The best a painter can hope
to accomplish is to fix the mood of an instant, the
momentary aspect of something. If he suggests
actual movement he must do it by palpable tricks,
all of which belong to craftsmanship rather than
to art. The work that he produces is comparable
to a single chord in music, without preparation or
resolution. It may be beautiful, but its beauty
plainly does not belong to the highest order. The
senses soon tire of such beauty. If a man stands
before a given painting for more than five or ten
minutes, it is usually a sign of affectation: he is
trying to convince himself that he has more delicate
perceptions than the general. Or he is a painter
himself and thus engrossed by the technical aspects
of it, as a plumber might be engrossed by the technical aspects of a bathroom. Or he is enchanted by
the story that the picture tells, which is to say, by
the literature that it illustrates. True enough, he
may go back to a painting over and over again, just
as a music-lover may strike and re-strike a chord
that pleases him, but it can't hold him for long at
one session—it can't move his feelings so powerfully that he forgets the real world he lives in.

Sculpture is in measurably better case. The spectator, viewing a fine statue, does not see something
dead, embalmed and fixed in a frame; he sees something that moves as he moves. A fine statue, in

other words, is not one statue, but hundreds, perhaps even thousands. The transformation from one to another is infinitely pleasing; one gets out of it the same satisfying stimulation that one gets out of the unrolling of a string quartette, or out of such a poem as "Atalanta in Calydon," "Heart of Darkness" or "Faust." So with architecture. It not only revolves; it also moves vertically, as the spectator approaches it. When one walks up a street past a beautiful building one certainly gets an effect beyond that of a mere chord; it is the effect of a whole procession of beautiful chords, like that at the beginning of the slow movement of the "New World" symphony or that in the well-known and much-battered Chopin prélude. If it were a painting it would soon grow tedious. No one, after a few days, would give it a glance.

This intrinsic hollowness of painting has its effects even upon those who most vigorously defend it as the queen of all the fine arts. One hears of such persons "haunting the galleries," but one always discovers, on inquiry, that it is the show-rooms that they actually haunt. In other words, they get their chief pleasure by looking at an endless succession of *new* paintings: the multitude of chords produces, in the end, a sort of confused satisfaction. One never hears of them going to a public gallery regularly, to look at this or that masterpiece. Even the Louvre seldom attracts them more than a dozen or so times in a life-time. The other arts make a far more powerful and permanent appeal. I have read "Huckleberry Finn" at least twenty times and "Typhoon" probably ten times, and yet both pleased me as much (nay, more) the last time as they did the first time. I have heard each of the first eight symphonies of Beethoven more than fifty times, and most of Mozart's, Haydn's, Schubert's and Schumann's quite as often. Yet if Beethoven's C Minor were announced for performance tonight, I'd surely go to hear it. More, I'd enjoy every instant of it. Even second-rate music has this lasting quality. Some time ago I heard Johann Strauss' waltz, "Geschichten aus dem Wiener Wald," for the first time in a long while. I knew it well in my goatish days; every note of it was still familiar. Nevertheless, it gave me exquisite delight. Imagine a man getting exquisite delight out of a painting of corresponding calibre—a painting already so familiar to him that he could reproduce it from memory!

Painters, like barbers and cigarmakers, are able to talk while they are at work, and so they commonly gabble about their art a great deal more than other artists, and the world, in consequence, has come to assume that it is very complex, and full of subtleties. This is not true. Most of its so-called subtleties are manufactured by painters who cannot paint.

The genuinely first-rate painters of the world have little to say about the technique of their art, and seem to be unaware that it is difficult. Go back to Leonardo's notes and sketches: you will find him a great deal more interested in anatomy than in painting. In fact, painting was a sort of afterthought with him; he was primarily an engineer, and the engineering that fascinated him most was that of the human body. Come down, then, to Cézanne. He painted in the way that seemed most natural to him, and was greatly astonished when a group of bad painters, seeking to imitate him, began crediting him with a long string of more or less mystical theories, by the Boul' Mich' out of the article on optics in the Encyclopædia Britannica.

The earliest Paleolithic men were already accomplished painters and sculptors. H. G. Wells, in his "Outline of History," says that "they drew astonishingly well." "Paint," he goes on, "was a big fact in their lives. They were inveterate painters." These savages were so low that they had not even invented bows and arrows, usury, the gallows or the notion of baptism by total immersion, and yet they were already accomplished draftsmen. Some of their drawings on the walls of their caves, indeed, remain a great deal more competent that the average magazine illustration of today. They also carved in stone and modelled in clay, and no doubt they were ac-

complished poets, as are the lowest Zuñi Indians of
our own time. Moreover, they soon began to move
out of their caves into artificial houses, and the principles of architectural design that they devised at
the very dawn of history have been unchanged ever
since, and are poll-parroted docilely every time a
sky-scraper thrusts its snout among the cherubim.
True enough, they could not draw as accurately as
a photographic lens, but they could certainly draw
as accurately as, say, Matisse or Gauguin. It remained for modern physicists, *i. e.*, men disdainful
of drawing, to improve it. All the progress that has
been made in the art during the past fifty or sixty
years has been based upon quiet filches from the
camera, just as all the progress that has been made
in painting has been based upon filches from the
spectroscope. When one finds a painter who professes to disdain these scientific aids, one always
beholds a painter who is actually unable to draw or
paint, and who seeks to conceal his incompetence
by clothing it in hocus-pocus. This is the origin of
the new art that regales us with legs eight feet long,
complexions of olive green, and human heads related to the soap-box rather than to the Edam cheese.
This is the origin of all the gabble one hears in ratty
and unheated studios about cubism, vortism, futur-
ism and other such childish follies.

I regard any human being who, with proper instruction, cannot learn to draw reasonably well as, to all intents and purposes, a moron. He is in a stage of culture actually anterior to that of the Crô-Magnons. As for a human being incapable of writing passable verse, he simply does not exist. It is done, as everyone knows, by children—and sometimes so well that their poems are printed in books and quite solemnly reviewed. But good music is never written by children—and I am not forgetting Mozart, Schubert and Mendelssohn. Music belongs to the very latest stage of culture; to compose it in the grand manner requires long and painful training, and the highest sort of natural skill. It is complex, delicate, difficult. A miraculous youth may show talent for it, but he never reaches anything properly describable as mastery of it until he is thoroughly mature. The music that all of us think of when we think of the best was written by men a bit bent by experience; it is quite beyond the comprehension of the general. And so with prose. Prose has no stage scenery to hide behind, as poetry has. It cannot use masks and wigs. It is not naïve, but infinitely sophisticated. It is not spontaneous, but must be fabricated by thought and painstaking. Prose is the ultimate flower of the art of words. Next to music, it is the finest of all the fine arts.

To return to music, it must be plain that it is enormously handicapped as an art by the mere fact that its technique is so frightfully difficult. I do not refer, of course, to the technique of the musical executant, but to that of the composer. Any literate man can master the technique of poetry in ten days, and that of the drama—despite all the solemn hocus-pocus of the professors who presume to teach it—in three weeks, but not even the greatest genius could do sound work in the sonata form without years of preparation. To write a good string quartette is not merely an act of creation, like writing a love song; it is also an act of applied science, like cutting out a set of tonsils. I know of no other art that demands so elaborate a professional training. Perhaps the one which comes nearest to it is architecture—that is, modern architecture. As the Greeks practised it, it was relatively simple, for they used simple materials and avoided all delicate problems of stress and strain; and they were thus able to keep their whole attention upon pure design. But the modern architect, with his complex mathematical and mechanical problems, must be an engineer before he is an artist, and the sort of engineering that he must master bristles with technical snares and conundrums. The serious musician is in even worse case. Before he may write at all he must take in and coördinate a body of technical knowledge that is almost as great as the outfit of an astronomer. I say that all this constitutes a handicap on the art of music.   What I mean is that it scares off many men who have sound musical ideas and would make good composers, but who have no natural talent or taste for the technical groundwork.   For one Schubert who overcomes the handicap by sheer genius there must be dozens who are repelled and discouraged.   There is another, and perhaps even worse disadvantage.   The potential Schuberts flee in alarm, but the Professor Sawdusts march in bravely.   That is to say, music is hard for musicians, but easy for pedants, grinds and examination-passers.   Its constant invasion by a hollow formalism is the result. It offers an inviting playground to the bombastic jackass whose delight it is to astonish the bourgeoisie with insane feats of virtuosity.

3

Symbiosis and the Artist

In contemplating the stupendous achievements of such a man as Wagner—achievements so colossal that only a small minority of men, specially trained, can even comprehend and appreciate them—one often finds one's self wondering how much further he would have gone had he not been harassed by his two wives.   His first wife, Minna Planer, was frankly and implacably opposed to his life-work, and made deliberate efforts to dissuade him from it. She regarded "Lohengrin" as nonsensical and "Tannhäuser" as downright indecent. It was her constant hope, until Wagner finally kicked her out, that he would give over such stuff, and consecrate himself to the composition of respectable operas in the manner of Rossini, her favorite composer. The only composition of his that genuinely pleased her was a set of variations for the *cornet à piston* that he wrote in Paris. She was a singer, and had the brains of one. It must be plain that the presence of such a woman—and Wagner lived with her for twenty years —must have put a fearful burden upon the man's creative genius. No man can be absolutely indifferent to the prejudices and opinions of his wife. She has too many opportunities to shove them down his throat. If she can't make him listen to them by howling and bawling, she can make him listen by snuffling. To say that he can carry on his work without paying any heed to her is equal to saying that he can carry on his work without paying any heed to his toothache, his conscience, or the boiler-factory next door. In spite of Minna, Wagner composed a number of very fine music dramas. But if he had poisoned her at the beginning of his career it is very likely that he would have composed more of them, and perhaps even better ones.

His second wife, the celebrated Cosima Liszt-von

Bülow, had far more intelligence than Minna, and so we may assume that her presence in his music factory was less of a handicap upon the composer. Nevertheless, the chances are that she, too, did him far more harm than good. To begin with, she was extremely plair in face—and nothing is more damaging to the creative faculty than the constant presence of ugliness. Cosima, in fact, looked not unlike a modern woman politician; even Nietzsche, a very romantic young fellow, had to go crazy before he could fall in love with her. In the second place, there is good reason to believe that Cosima, until after Wagner's death, secretly believed that her father, Papa Liszt, was a far better musician. Men's wives almost invariably make some such mistake; to find one who can separate the man of genius from the mere husband, and then estimate the former accurately and fairly, is surely very rare. A woman usually respects her father, but her view of her husband is mingled with contempt, for she is of course privy to the transparent devices by which she snared him. It is difficult for her, being so acutely aware of the shallowness of the man, to give due weight to the dignity of the artist. Moreover, Cosima had shoddy tastes, and they played destructively upon poor Wagner. There are parts of "Parsifal" that suggest her very strongly—more strongly, in fact, than they suggest the author of "Die Götterdämmerung." I do not here decry Wagner; on the contrary, I praise him, and perhaps excessively. It is staggering to think of the work he did, with Minna and Cosima shrilling into his ears. What interests me is the question as to how much further he might have gone had he escaped the passionate affection of the two of them and of their various volunteer assistants. The thought fascinates, and almost alarms. There is a limit beyond which sheer beauty becomes unseemly. In "Tristan und Isolde," in the Ring, and even in parts of "Parsifal," Wagner pushes his music very near that limit. A bit beyond lies the fourth dimension of tone—and madness. Both Beethoven and Brahms, I believe, more than once edged over the line. Two bachelors. Had Beethoven married in 1802, as he seems to have been tempted to do by some scheming wench, it is doubtful that the world would ever have heard the Eroica. In the Eroica there is everything that startles and dismays a loving wife: brilliant novelty, vast complexity, thunderous turmoil, great bursts of undiluted genius. Even Beethoven never wrote anything more astounding than its first movement; the first movement of the C Minor is relatively elemental beside it. Nor is there anything so revolutionary in the Ninth.

The Eroica, indeed, was written precisely at the moment when Beethoven became fully conscious of his extraordinary powers—more accurately, of his singular and unchallengeable *superiority*. It is the work, not only of a man who is absolute master of his materials, but also of a man who disdains his materials, and his customers with them. In the first movement he simply spits into the face of the cosmos. Scarcely ten measures have been played before one suddenly realizes that one is in the presence of something entirely new in music—not merely new in degree, but new in kind. It differs as much from anything written before it, even by Beethoven, as a picture by Cézanne differs from a picture by an English Academician. This first movement has never been sufficiently studied and appraised: it is unutterably stupendous. In the funeral march, I believe, Beethoven descends to some rather cheap tricks, and in the scherzo he is often obvious. But in the first movement, and to a slightly less degree in the last, he takes leave of earth and disports himself among the gods. It is the composition of a colossus. And a bachelor. No normal woman could have watched its genesis without some effort to make it more seemly, more decorous and connubial, more respectable. A faithful wife, present at its first performance, would have blushed, shivered and sworn. Women hate revolutions and revolutionists. They like men who are docile, and well-regarded at the bank, and never late at meals.

XV. CONTRIBUTIONS TO THE STUDY OF VULGAR PSYCHOLOGY

1

The Downfall of the Navy

FEW phenomena offer more refined and instructive entertainment to the psychic pathologist than the American navy's decline in popularity during the past twenty-five years. At the time of the Spanish-American War, as everyone sentient in those days will recall, it was easily the premier service in the popular regard, and in even the least of its exploits the great masses of the plain people took a violent and vociferous pride. They were proud, too, of the army, and its heroic efforts against the Hunnish hordes of Spain, and one of the great captains of that army was made President for his stupendous feats of blood and blather in the field; but it was the navy that they cherished most, and the popular heroes that it produced were more numerous than those of the army, and in the main they were far more fondly cherished. Even the im-

mortal Roosevelt, it will be remembered, was half a
navy man, and what got him into the White House,
I believe, was less his colossal butcheries in the land
battles of the war, important though they were to the
cause of human liberty, than his long antecedent
struggles to free the navy from the politicians, and
make it fit to fight.   The navy, indeed, was popular
before the war began, or even threatened.   The army
could tackle and massacre a whole tribe of Indians
without causing half the public thrill that followed
the bombardment of a Venezuelan coast village by
the White Squadron, with a total loss of but one blind
cripple crippled in the other leg.   This White Squadron, I more than suspect, was the actual cause of
the war itself.   From the day it first put to sea the
plain people watched it with glowing pride, and
longed for a sight of it in action.   If it had not been
so handily cruising in Latin-American waters, glittering truculently in the sunshine, there would have
been a great deal less public indignation over the
wrongs of the Cubeens.   So superb a fighting arm
was surely not designed by God to rust in the scab-
bard.   Thus the fashion arose of drawing it out and
poking it into Caribbean and South Atlantic rat-
holes.   During the half dozen years before the laying of the Spanish dragon was formally undertaken,
such heroes as Schley and Fighting Bob Evans carried the White Squadron into half the ports to the

southward, and knocked over a few church steeples in most of them. In the end, it was just such an enterprise that took the *Maine* into Havana harbor, and provided the legal excuse for the war itself.

This was more than a quarter of a century ago. Today, it must be obvious that there is very little public pride in the navy, and almost no public interest. I doubt that one American schoolboy out of ten thousand could name its present ranking officer; between 1890 and 1900 every schoolboy knew all the admirals by face and by name, and most of the captains, and the patriotic epigrams of the more articulate of them were chalked upon every schoolyard fence in the land. I was myself a boy in those days, and remember even today such forgotten heroes of the time as Admiral Gherardi, who commanded the White Squadron in 1893 and 1894, and was retired before the Spanish War; his portrait was on the cigarette cards, along with those of Fighting Bob Evans and Lillian Russell. Later on, having grown more reflective and critical, I specialized in the Sampson-Schley controversy, and was a bitter partisan of Schley, a native of my own Maryland Free State. Dewey, Clark, Evans, Ridley, Hobson (God save us!), Ensign Bagley, Yoeman Ellis, Sigsbee, Wainright—all these eminent tars were as real to the boys of that era as John L. Sullivan or Amos Rusie. Turn now to today. When the newspapers, a year or two ago, announced that a gentleman named Admiral Sims had denied that the German U-boat commanders committed the atrocities credited to them during the late war, how many American boys recognized his name? I myself, though I am a historian by profession, boggled him at first glance, mistaking him for a British officer. For the life of me, I could not tell you the name of another American naval officer. . . . Second thought: there was Admiral Benson. But what he did in the war, save involve himself in some controversy that has been forgotten, I can't tell you. No other name occurs to me, though I scratch my head and try various mnemonic dodges. Try me on the names of the commanders who fought the celebrated Creel battle with the U-boats, and I'll have to slide down among the morons. If there was a Hobson in that war, I can't recall him. I remember many English and German commanders—von Tirpitz, von Scheer, Jellicoe, Müller of the Emden, König, and so on—but not a single American.

The fact is, of course, that the part the American navy played in the war, though it was unquestionably important, was quite devoid of the more spectacular varieties of gallantry, and so it failed to make heroes. The battles fought were fought mainly by government press-agents, not by the navy itself; the rest was dangerous but dull policing, with some uninspiring running of ferry-boats. The navy, as everyone knows, became a funk-hole for draft-dodgers. This may account, in some measure, for the present public apathy regarding it; it is not brilliant, and hence it is not charming. But its decay in popularity, I believe, really antedated the war by several years; it was in the shadows long before Admiral Sims transferred his swivel-chair from Washington to London. What caused the change? Is it that the American people have lost their old taste for the sea, and, in particular, their old delight in the sort of heroes that it produces? Or is it that the navy itself has actually lost some of its old romance and color? I incline to think that the latter explanation explains more than the former. My hazard is that the man who made the American navy unpopular was the Hon. Josephus Daniels, and that he did it by trying to convert every battleship into a chautauqua and Sunday-school. In the days when the arrival of a naval vessel in port was the signal for hot times ashore, with the saloons packed to the doors, and all the town's wicked women out *en masse,* and the streets made picturesquely perilous by squads of drunken and roaring gobs—in those days every poor but ambitious boy, when the job of tying up packages and running errands began to palsy him, let his fancy turn toward thoughts of stealing off to foreign parts, the Republic's quarter in his pocket and riotous

and attractive company all about him.   The sailor
of that era was an obscene but highly charming fellow.   A great spaciousness was in him.   He bore
the scars of the constabulary espantoons of distant
and romantic lands.   He was a wholesale lover, a
three-bottle man, a well of astounding profanity.
He held the admiration of every adventurous youth.
He was romance in baggy breeches, hell-bent down
the mysterious by-ways of the world.

Josephus changed all that.   A Christian of tender
conscience and a firm believer in hell for the sinful,
it appalled him to observe that nine-tenths of the
young men under his official charge were obviously
headed for the fire.   When he got his secret reports
of their doings in Port Said, Callao, Singapore,
Odessa, Smyrna, Vera Cruz, Norfolk, Va., and other
such seaboard stews—when these lurid documents
began pouring in upon him from missionaries,
Y. M. C. A. secretaries and other godly men, he staggered under the horror, and was unfit for business
for days afterward.   Having recourse to prayer, he
was presently given counsel by a voice from the
burning bush.   To hear was to act.   First, he
abolished rum from the navy, and forced even the
oldest admirals, some of whom had been pickled
for years and years, to go upon the dubious water
of far-flung and zymotic ports.   Secondly, he for-
bade the enlistment of young men who were fugitives

from justice for dog-stealing, moonshining, window-smashing and other such felonies—the mainstays of the navy in the old days. Thirdly, he set up night schools on every battleship, in charge of Christian men like himself, and then day schools, and then schools running both day and night, and to the customary instruction in the three R's he added the whole curriculum of the Y. M. C. A., from double-entry bookkeeping to public speaking, and from show-card writing to venereal prophylaxis. Today a young man goes into the navy from his native farm with nothing in his head save a vast yearning to get away from the smell of cows—and comes out in three years an accomplished paperhanger, with some knowledge of the saxophone, electric wiring and first aid to the injured. The old enlistment posters used to show a gob in a rickshaw with a Japanese cutie; the new ones show him practising as a house and sign painter. The old navy showed the boys the world, and taught them the difference between Swedish punch and Javanese arrak; the new navy converts them into sanitary plumbers and book-keepers, and teaches them how to lead a prayer-meeting.

Is it any wonder that it declines in popularity—that the youth of the land is neglectful of its eminent commanders, and has to be lured into enlistments by the arts of the grind-shop auctioneer? The

Y. M. C. A. already reigns universally on the dry land of the Republic; only the remotest yokel in the highest hills can hope to escape its tentacles, and even he is fetched by its sinister sister, the chautauqua. When he dreams of the sea, he dreams of a realm that is free from all this—of a realm still barbarous, unchastened and romantic—a realm of free cavorting and exhilarating adventure.   But when he gets to the recruiting-office, the first thing he sees is a large lithograph showing a class of gobs being instructed in algebra, grammar and Christian doctrine.   The master-at-arms who receives him hasn't got the old naked Venus tattooed on his arm; he has instead a portrait of Dwight L. Moody, and in his button-hole is a button testifying that he has recited 52 successive Golden Texts without an error and brought 20 heathen Danish sailors to the mourners' bench.   Instead of the old booby-hatch for souses in this recruiting-office, there is now a gospel hall with a melodeon.   The talk is not of the yellow gals in Valparaiso, the powerful red wines of Naples, the all-night shows of Marseilles, the police of Liverpool and Kiel, but of the advantages of learning the trades of tin-roofer, cost accountant and hardwood finisher.   The rustic candidate, his head buzzing with romance, is floored with statistics and plunged into a bath of bichloride of mercury.   No wonder his stomach turns and his heart is broken!   And no wonder the navy, thus purged of all its old flavors and juices, has ceased to inflame the imagination of the plain people. Suppose they heard from Hollywood that Charlie Chaplin had become a hard-shell Baptist and opened a pants-pressing parlor?

2

The Mind of the Slave

One of the forgotten divisions between men and men is that separating those who enjoy the work they have to do in the world and those who suffer it only as a necessary evil. The distinction, despite its neglect by sociologists, is probably very important— certainly far more important than the current divisions between producers and exploiters, dolichocephalic Nordic blonds and brachycephalic Alpines, Darwinians and so-called Christians, Republicans and Democrats, Protestants and Catholics, wets and drys. A man's politics, theology and other vices engage his attention, after all, only in his moments of leisure, and the shape of his cranium has very little demonstrable influence upon what habitually goes on within it, but the nature of the work he does in the world conditions every thought and impulse of his life, and his general attitude toward it is almost indistinguishable from his general attitude toward the cosmos.

At the one extreme lies the unmitigated slave—the man who has to spend his whole life performing tasks that are incurably uninteresting, and that offer no soothing whatever to his vanity.   At the other extreme is what Beethoven called the free artist—the man who makes a living, with no boss directly over him, doing things that he enjoys enormously, and that he would keep on doing gladly, even if all economic pressure upon him disappeared.   To the second category belong all the happiest men in the world, and hence, perhaps, all the most useful men.   For what is done with joy is always better done, whether it be fashioning a material object, thinking out a problem or kissing a pretty girl; and the man who can make the rest of humanity pay him for being happy is obviously a better man than the general, or, at all odds, a luckier one.   Here luck and superiority are one and the same.   The fact that Joseph Conrad could write better than I, was in a sense, a matter of pure chance.   He was born with his talent; he did not earn it.   Nevertheless, it was just as real as if he had got it by Christian endeavor, and his superiority to me was thus perfectly genuine.

The slave is always conscious of his slavery, and makes constant and often desperate efforts to mitigate it or to get rid of it altogether.   Sometimes he seeks that mitigation in outside activities that promise to give him the sense of dignity and importance that his daily labor denies him; sometimes he tries to give a false appearance of dignity to his work itself. The last phenomenon must be familiar to every American; it is responsible for various absurd devices to pump up lowly trades by giving them new and high-sounding names. I point, for example, to those of the real-estate agent and the undertaker. Neither trade, it must be obvious, offers any stimulation to men of genuine superiority. One could not imagine a Beethoven, a Lincoln or even a Coolidge getting any joy out of squeezing apartment-house tenants or pickling Odd Fellows. Both jobs, indeed, fail to satisfy the more imaginative sort of men among those compelled to practise them. Hence these men try to dignify them with hocus-pocus. The real-estate agent, seeking to conceal his real purpose in life, lets it be known grandly that he is an important semi-public functionary, that he has consecrated himself to Service and is a man of Vision—and to prove it he immerses himself in a private office with a secretary to insult his customers, joins a Rotary Club, and begins to call himself a realtor, a word as idiotic as flu, pep or gent. The ambitious washer of the dead—until very lately a sort of pariah in all civilized societies, like the hangman, the surgeon and the dog-catcher—proceeds magnificently along the same route. At regular intervals I receive impressive literature from a trade-union of undertakers calling

themselves the Selected Morticians. By this literature it appears that the members thereof are professional men of a rank and dignity comparable to
judges or archbishops, and they are hot for the
subtlest and most onerous kind of Service, and even
eager to offer their advice to the national government.
In brief, the realtor complex all over again. I do
not laugh at these soaring embalmers; I merely point
out that their nonsense proves how little the mere
planting of martyred lodge brothers satisfies their
interior urge to be important and distinguished—
an urge that is in all of us.

But most of the trades pursued by slaves, of course,
offer no such opportunities for self-deceptive flum-
mery. The clerk working in the lime and cement
warehouse of some remote town of the foreign mis-
sions belt cannot conceivably convince himself that
his profession is noble; worse, he cannot convince
anyone else. And so with millions of other men in
this great Republic, both urban and rural—millions
of poor fellows doomed their life long to dull, stupid
and tedious crafts—the lower sort of clerks, workmen, wagon-drivers, farmers, farm-laborers, petty
officials, grabbers of odd jobs. They must be downright idiots to get any satisfaction out of their work.
Happiness, the feeling that they too are somebody,
the sense of being genuinely alive, must be sought in
some other direction. In the big cities, that need is

easily met. Here there is a vast and complex machinery for taking the slave's mind off his desolate-
ness of spirit—moving pictures to transport him into
a land of romance, where men (whom he always
identifies with himself) are brave, rich and hand-
some, and women (whom he identifies with his wife
—or perchance with her younger sister) are clean,
well-dressed and beautiful; newspapers to delight
and instruct him with their sports pages, their comic
strips and their eloquent appeals to his liberality,
public spirit and patriotism; public bands and the
radio to play the latest jazz for him; circuses and
parades; baseball, races, gambling, harlotry and
games in arenas; a thousand devices to make him
forget his woes. It is this colossal opportunity to
escape from life that brings yokels swarming to the
cities, not any mere lust for money. The yokel is
actually far more comfortable on his native soil; the
city crowds and exploits him, and nine times out of
ten he remains desperately poor. But the city at
least teaches him how to forget his poverty; it amuses
him and thrills him while it is devouring him. I
once knew an old colored woman, born in Southern
Maryland, who lived miserably in one room of a
shack in an alley in Baltimore. When asked why she
did not go back to her village, where she would have
at least had better food and more air, she replied very
simply that there were never any parades in the

country.   It was a profound and intelligent saying.

But millions of the slaves, of course, must remain in the small towns or on the land; the cities can't absorb all of them, nor even half of them.   They thus confront the problem of making life bearable out of their own meagre resources.   The devices that they adopt—political, religious and social—are familiar to all of us, and account fully, it seems to me, for some of the phenomena of American life that are most puzzling to foreign observers.   The hoop-la Methodist revival with its psychopathological basis; the violent bitterness of rural politics; the prosperity of the Ku Klux Klan and all the other clownish fraternal orders; the persistent popularity of lynching, tarring and feathering, barbarities of a dozen other varieties—all these things are no more than manifestations of the poor hind's pathetic effort to raise himself out of his wallow, to justify and dignify his existence, to escape from the sordid realities that daily confront him.   To snort and froth at a revival makes him conspicuous, prominent, a man of mark; it is therefore easy to induce him to do it.   To hold a petty county office is eminence; hence he struggles for it frantically.   To belong to the Ku Klux gives him a mysterious and sinister dignity, and fills him with a sense of power and consequence; he falls for it as quickly as a city intellectual falls for the *Légion*

d'honneur or an LL.D. To take a hand in a concrete tarring or lynching—this instantly makes him
feel that he has played an heroic rôle in the world,
that he has accomplished something large and mem-
orable—above all, that he has had a gaudy good time.
In brief, all these things make him forget, transiently
or permanently, that he is a miserable worm, and
of little more actual importance on earth than his
own hogs.

Long ago, I suggested that a good way to diminish
lynching in the South would be to establish brass
bands in all the country towns. The bad music, I
argued, would engage and enchant both the blacka-
moors and the poor white trash, and so discourage the
former from crime and the latter from seeking a
savage satisfaction in its punishment. I now improve and embellish that suggestion. That is to say,
I propose that the band scheme be shelved, and that
bull-fighting be established as a substitute. Why
not, indeed? Cattle have to be killed, and the
Southern poor white is admittedly a savage. Why
not combine the necessary slaughter of horned quad-
rupeds with a show that will give that savage a thrill
and take his mind from his lowly lot, and so turn
him from seeking escape in politics, murder and
voodoo theology? Bull-fights in the South would not
only diminish lynchings; they would also undermine

Prohibition.   A happy peasantry would have no reason to divert itself with homicide, and neither would it
have any reason to belabor the rest of us with the ethical and political manias of its Baptist dervishes.   The
Ku Klux, it seems to me, is a good influence in the
South rather than a bad one, for it tends to regulate
and formalize the normal sports of the people, and so
restrains excess.   The trouble with lynching before
the Klan took charge of it was that men of the darker
races were often hanged and burned purely arbitrarily, simply because the yokels of some Christian
county could not stand boredom any longer.   But
now rules are laid down and a sort of jurisprudence
gets into it.   I have heard all kinds of wild charges
against the Invisible Empire, but I have never heard
anyone allege that its responsible officers have ever
countenanced the execution of its laws upon anyone
not obviously guilty.   This is an improvement.   Life
is safer and happier in Georgia today that it was before the Rev. Dr. Simmons heard the voice.   But it
would be even safer and even happier if the pure
Anglo-Saxons down there could work off their steam
by going weekly to a *plaza de toros,* and there see
official *picadores, banderilleros,* and *matadors,* all
of them good Democrats and baptized men, lynch
and burn (or even merely geld) a reluctant and protesting male of *Bos taurus.*

3

The Art Eternal

One of the laudable by-products of the Freudian necromancy is the discovery that lying, in most cases, is involuntary and inevitable—that the liar can no more avoid it than he can avoid blinking his eyes when a light flashes or jumping when a bomb goes off behind him. At its worst, indeed, this necessity takes on a downright pathological character, and is thus as innocent as sciatica or albuminuria. It is part of the morbid baggage of hysterics and neurasthenics: their lying is simply a symptom of their compulsive effort to adjust themselves to an environment which bears upon them too harshly for endurance. The rest of us are not quite so hard pushed, but pushed we all are. In us the thing works through the inferiority complex, which no man can escape. He who lacks it entirely is actually reckoned insane by the fact: his satisfaction with his situation in the world is indistinguishable from a delusion of grandeur. The great majority of us—all, in brief, who are normal—pass through life in constant revolt against our limitations, objective and subjective. Our conscious thought is largely devoted to plans and specifications for cutting a better figure in human society, and in our unconscious the business goes on much more steadily and powerfully. No healthy man, in his secret heart, is content with his destiny. Even the late Woodrow, during his dizzy term as the peer of Lincoln and Washington, was obviously tantalized by the reflection that, in earlier ages, there had been Martin Luther, St. Ignatius Loyola and Paul of Tarsus. We are tortured by such dreams and images as a child is tortured by the thought of a state of existence in which it would live in a candystore and have two stomachs. The more we try to put the obscene apparition away, the more it haunts and badgers us.

Lying is the product of the unconscious yearning to realize such visions, and if the policeman, conscience, prevents the lie being put into plain words, then it is at least put into more or less plausible acts. We all play parts when we face our fellow-men, as even poets have noticed. No man could bring himself to reveal his true character, and, above all, his true limitations as a citizen and a Christian, his true meannesses, his true imbecilities, to his friends, or even to his wife. Honest autobiography is therefore a contradiction in terms: the moment a man considers himself, even *in petto*, he tries to gild and fresco himself. Thus a man's wife, however realistic her view of him, always flatters him in the end, for the worst she sees in him is appreciably better, by the time she sees it, than what is actually there. What she sees, even at times of the most appalling domestic revelation and confidence, is not the authentic man at all, but a compound made up in part of the authentic man and in part of his projection of a gaudy ideal. The man who is most respected by his wife is the one who makes this projection most vivid—that is, the one who is the most daring and ingratiating liar. He can never, of course, deceive her utterly, but if he is skillful he may at least deceive her enough to make her happy.

Omnis homo mendax: thus the Psalmist. So far the Freudians merely parrot him. What is new in their gospel is the doctrine that lying is instinctive, normal, and unavoidable—that a man is forced into it by his very will-to-live. This doctrine purges the business of certain ancient embarrassments, and restores innocence to the heart. Think of a lie as a compulsion neurose, and you think of it more kindly. I need not add, I hope, that this transfer of it from the department of free will to that of determinism by no means disposes of the penalty that traditionally pursues it, supposing it to be detected and resented. The proponents of free will always make the mistake of assuming that the determinists are simply evil fellows looking for a way to escape the just consequences of their transgressing. No sense is in that assumption. If I lie on the witness-stand and am de-

tected by the judge, I am jailed for perjury forth-
with, regardless of my helplessness under compulsion.   Here justice refuses absolutely to distinguish
between a misfortune and a tort: the overt act is all
it is concerned with.   But as jurisprudence grows
more intelligent and more civilized it may change
its tune, to the benefit of liars, which is to say, to the
benefit of humanity.   Science is unflinchingly de-
terministic, and it has begun to force its determinism
into morals.   We no longer flog a child afflicted with
nocturnal enuresis; we have substituted concepts of
mental aberration for concepts of crime in a whole
series of cases: kleptomania-shoplifting, pyromania-
arson, etc.; and, in the United States at least, the old
savage punishment of murderers is now ameliorated
by considerations of psychiatry and even of honor.
On some shining tomorrow a psychoanalyst may be
put into the box to prove that perjury is simply a
compulsion neurose, like beating time with the foot
at a concert or counting the lamp-posts along the
highway.

However, I have but small faith in millenniums,
and do not formally predict this one.   Nor do I pronounce any moral judgment, pro or con: moral
judgments, as old Friedrich used to say, are foreign
to my nature.   But let us not forget that lying, *per
se,* is not forbidden by the moral code of Christendom.   Holy Writ dismisses it cynically, and the

statutes of all civilized states are silent about it.
Only the Chinese, indeed, make it a penal offense.
Perjury, of course, is prohibited everywhere, and also
any mendacity which amounts to fraud and deprives
a fellow-man of his property, but that far more common form of truth-stretching which has only the lesser
aim of augmenting the liar's personal dignity and
consequence—this is looked upon with a very char-
itable eye. So is that form which has the aim of
helping another person in the same way. In the
latter direction lying may even take on the stature
of a positive virtue. The late King Edward VII,
when Prince of Wales, attained to great popularity
throughout Christendom by venturing into downright
perjury. Summoned into a court of law to give expert testimony regarding some act of adultery, he
lied like a gentleman, as the phrase goes, to protect
a woman. The lie, to be sure, was intrinsically useless; no one believed that the lady was innocent.
Nevertheless, every decent Christian applauded the
perjurer for his good intentions, including even the
judge on the bench, sworn to combat false witness
by every resource of forensics. All of us, worms
that we are, occasionally face the alternatives that
confronted Edward. On the one hand, we may tell
the truth, regardless of consequences, and on the
other hand we may mellow it and sophisticate it to
make it humane and tolerable. It is universally held

that the man who chooses the first course is despicable. He may be highly moral, but he is nevertheless a cad—as highly moral men have so curious a way of being. But if he lies boldly, then he is held to be a man of honor, and is respected as such by all other men of honor.

For the habitual truth-teller and truth-seeker, indeed, the world has very little liking. He is always unpopular, and not infrequently his unpopularity is so excessive that it endangers his life. Run your eye back over the list of martyrs, lay and clerical: nine-tenths of them, you will find, stood accused of nothing worse than honest efforts to find out and announce the truth. Even today, with the scientific passion become familiar in the world, the general view of such fellows is highly unfavorable. The typical scientist, the typical critic of institutions, the typical truth-seeker in every field is held under suspicion by the great majority of men, and variously beset by posses of relentless foes. If he tries to find out the truth about arterio-sclerosis, or surgical shock, or cancer, he is denounced as a scoundrel by the Christian Scientists, the osteopaths and the anti-vivisectionists. If he tries to tell the truth about the government, its agents seek to silence him and punish him. If he turns to fiction and endeavors to depict his fellow-men accurately, he has the Comstocks on his hands. In no field can he count upon a friendly audience, and freedom from assault. Especially in the United States is his whole enterprise viewed with bilious eye. The men the American people admire most extravagantly are the most daring liars; the men they detest most violently are those who try to tell them the truth. A Galileo could no more be elected President of the United States than he could be elected Pope of Rome. Both high posts are reserved for men favored by God with an extraordinary genius for swathing the bitter facts of life in bandages of soft illusion.

Behind this almost unanimous distrust of the truth-teller there is a sound and sure instinct, as there is behind every other manifestation of crowd feeling. What it shows is simply this: that the truth is something too harsh and devastating for the majority of men to bear. In their secret hearts they know themselves, and they can suffer the thought of themselves only by idealizing the facts. The more trivial, loathsome and degraded the reality, the more powerful and relentless must be the idealization. An Aristotle, I daresay, may be able occasionally to regard himself searchingly and dispassionately—but certainly not an ordinary man. Here we come back to what we began with: the inferiority complex. The truth-seeker forgets it, and so comes to grief. He forgets that the ordinary man, at bottom, is always afraid of himself, as of some horrible monster. He refuses to sanction the lie whereby the ordinary man maintains his self-respect, just as the bounder, put upon the stand, refuses to support the lie whereby a woman maintains the necessary theory of her chastity. Thus he is unpopular, and deserves to be.

Then why does he go on? Why does he kick up such a bother and suffer such barbarous contumely, all to no end—for the majority of so-called truths, it must be evident, perish as soon as they are born: no one will believe them. The answer probably is that the truth-seeker is moved by the same obscure inner necessity (in Joseph Conrad's phrase) that animates the artist. Something within him, something entirely beyond his volition, forces him to pursue his fanatical and useless quest—some impulse as blind as that which moves a puppy to chase its tail. Again the compulsion neurose! But this one differs materially from that of the liar. The latter is hygienic; it makes for peace, health, happiness. The former makes only for strife and discontent. It invades the immemorial pruderies of the human race. It breeds scandals and heart-burnings. It is essentially anti-social, and hence, by modern theories of criminology, diseased. The truth-seeker thus becomes a pathological case. The average man is happily free from any such malaise. He avoids the truth as diligently as he avoids arson, regicide or piracy on the high seas, and for the same reason: because he believes that it is dangerous, that no good can come of it, that it doesn't pay. The very thought of it is abhorrent to him. This average man, I believe, must be accepted as the normal man, the natural man, the healthy and useful man. He presents a character that is general in the race, and favorable to its security and contentment. The truth never caresses; it stings—and life is surely too short for sane men to be stinging themselves unnecessarily. One would regard it as idiotic even in a flea.

Thus the truth about the truth emerges, and with it the truth about lying. Lying is not only excusable; it is not only innocent, and instinctive; it is, above all, necessary and unavoidable. Without the ameliorations that it offers life would become a mere syllogism, and hence too metallic to be born. The man who lies simply submits himself sensibly to the grand sweep and ripple of the cosmic process. The man who seeks and tells the truth is a rebel against the inner nature of all of us.

XVI. THE AMERICAN NOVEL

1

IT is an ancient platitude of historical criticism that great wars and their sequelæ are inimical to the fine arts, and particularly to the art of letters. The kernel of truth in it lies in the obvious fact that a people engaged in a bitter struggle for existence have no time for such concerns, which demand not only leisure but also a certain assured feeling of security, well-being and self-sufficiency—in brief, the thing often called aristocratic (or sometimes intellectual) detachment. No man ever wrote good poetry with his wife in parturition in the next room, or the police preparing to raid his house, or his shirt-tail afire. He needs to be comfortable to do it, and if not actually comfortable, then at all events safe. Wars tend to make life uncomfortable and unsafe—but not, it must be observed, inevitably and necessarily, not always and invariably. A bitter and demoralizing struggle goes with wars that are lost, and the same struggle goes with wars that are won only by dint of stupendous and ruinous effort, but it certainly does not go with wars that are won easily.

These last do not palsy and asphyxiate the artist, as he is palsied and asphyxiated by cholera morbus, suits for damages or marriage. On the contrary, they pump him full of ozone, and he is never more alive and lively than following them.

I point to a few familiar examples. The Civil War, as everyone knows, bankrupted the South and made a life a harsh and bitter struggle for its people, and especially for the gentler and more civilized minority of its people. In consequence, the South became as sterile artistically, after Lee's surrender, as Mexico or Portugal, and even today it lags far behind the North in beautiful letters, and even further behind in music, painting and architecture. But the war, though it went on for four years, strained the resources of the North very little, either in men or in money, and so its conclusion found the Northerners very rich and cocky, and full of a yearning to astonish the world, and that yearning, in a few decades, set up a new and extremely vigorous American literature, created an American architecture of a revolutionary character, and even laid the first courses of American schools of music and painting. Mark Twain, Walt Whitman, Henry James and William Dean Howells, all of them draft dodgers in the war itself, were in a very real sense products of the war, for they emerged as phenomena of the great outburst of creative energy that followed it, and all of them, including even James, were as thoroughly American as Jay Gould, P. T. Barnum or Jim Fisk. The stars of the national letters in the years before the war had been Americans only by geographical accident. About Emerson there hung a smell of Königsberg and Weimar; Irving was simply a New York Englishman; Poe was a citizen of No Man's Land; even Hawthorne and Cooper, despite their concern with American themes, showed not the slightest evidence of an American point of view. But Mark Twain, Howells and Whitman belonged to the Republic as palpably as Niagara Falls or Tammany Hall belonged to it, and so did James, though the thought horrified him and we must look at him through his brother William to get the proof. Turn now to Europe. France, harshly used in the war of 1870–71, was sterile for a decade, but the wounds were not deep, and recovery was in full swing by 1880. Germany, injured scarcely at all, produced Nietzsche almost before the troops got home, and was presently offering an asylum and an inspiration to Ibsen, preparing the way for the reform and modernization of the theatre, and making contributions of the utmost value to practically all of the arts and sciences. Spain, after the Armada, gave the world Cervantes and then expired; England produced Shakespeare and founded a literature that is not surpassed in history.

What has thus happened over and over again in the past—and I might pile up examples for pages—may be in process of repetition today, and under our very noses. All Europe, plainly enough, is in a state of exhaustion and depression, and in no department of human activity is the fact more visible than in that of the arts. Not only are the defeated nations, Russia, Germany and Austria, producing nothing save a few extravagant eccentricities; there is also a great lowness of spirit in the so-called victorious nations, for their victory was almost as ruinous as defeat. France, as after 1870, is running to a pretentious and artificial morbidity in letters, and marking time in music and painting; Italy is producing little save psychopathological absurdities by such mountebanks as D'Annunzio and Papini; even England shows all the signs of profound fatigue. The great English writers of the age before the war are passing. Meredith is gone; Hardy has put up his shutters; Kipling went to wreck in the war itself; Conrad is dead; Shaw, once so agile and diverting, becomes a seer and prophet. Nor is there any sign of sound progress among the younger men. Arnold Bennett, a star of brilliant promise in 1913, is today a smoking smudge. Wells has ceased to be an artist and become a prophet in the Sunday supplements. Masefield has got no further than he was on August 2, 1914. The rest of the novelists are simply chasing their own tails.   The Georgian poets, having emerged gloriously during the war, now disappear behind their manners.   Only a few women, led by May Sinclair, and a few iconoclastic young men, led by Aldous Huxley, are still indubitably alive.

It seems to me that, in the face of this dark depression across the water, the literary spectacle on this side takes on an aspect that is extremely reassuring, and even a bit exhilarating.   For the first time in history, there begins to show itself the faint shadow of a hope that, if all goes well, leadership in the arts, and especially in all the art of letters, may eventually transfer itself from the eastern shore of the Altantic to the western shore.   Our literature, as I have more than once pointed out in the past, is still oppressed by various heavy handicaps, chiefly resident in the failure of the new aristocracy of money to function as an aristocracy of taste.   The artist among us is still a sort of pariah, beset by public contempt on the one hand and by academic enmity on the other; he still lacks the public position that his brothers enjoy in older and more civilized countries. Nevertheless, it must be obvious to everyone that his condition tends to improve materially—that, in our own time, it *has* improved materially—that though his rewards remain meagre, save in mere money, his freedom grows steadily greater.   And it must be obvious, too, that he begins to show that

that increasing freedom is not wholly wasted upon him—that he knows how to use it, and is disposed to do so with some gusto. What all the younger American writers have in common is a sort of new-found elasticity or goatishness, a somewhat exaggerated sense of aliveness, a glowing delight in the spectacle before them, a vigorous and naïve self-consciousness. The schoolmaster critics belabor them for it, and call it a disrespect for tradition, and try to put it down by denouncing it as due to corrupt foreign influences. But it is really a proof of the rise of nationalism—perhaps of the first dawn of a genuine sense of nationality. No longer imitative and timorous, as most of their predecessors were, these youngsters are attempting a first-hand examination of the national scene, and making an effort to represent it in terms that are wholly American. They are the pioneers of a literature that, whatever its defects in the abstract, will at least be a faithful reflection of the national life, that will be more faithful, indeed, in its defects than in its merits. In England the novel subsides into formulæ, the drama is submerged in artificialities, and even poetry, despite occasional revolts, moves toward scholarliness and emptiness. But in America, since the war, all three show the artless and superabundant energy of little children. They lack, only too often, manner and urbanity; it is no wonder that they are often shocking to pedants.   But there is the breath of life in them, and that life is far nearer its beginning than its end.

The causes of all this are not far to seek.   The American Legion is right: we won the war.   It cost us nothing in men; it brought us a huge profit in money; as Europe has gone down, we have gone up. Moreover, it produced a vast discharge of spiritual electricity, otherwise and more injuriously dissipated in the countries more harshly beset.   The war was fought ignobly; its first and most obvious effect was to raise up a horde of cads, and set them in authority as spokesmen of the nation.   But out of that swinishness there was bound to come reaction, and out of the reaction there was bound to flow a desire to re-examine the whole national pretension—to turn on the light, to reject old formulæ, to think things out anew and in terms of reality.   Suddenly the old houses of cards came tumbling down, and the professors inhabiting them ran about in their night-shirts, bawling for the police.   The war, first and last, produced a great deal more than John Dos Passos' "Three Soldiers."   It also produced Lewis' "Babbitt," and Cabell's "Jurgen," and Fergusson's "Capitol Hill," and O'Neill's "The Emperor Jones." And, producing them, it ended an epoch of sweetness and light.

2

The young American literatus of today, with pub-lishers ready and eager to give him a hearing, can scarcely imagine the difficulties which beset his predecessor of twenty years ago; he is, indeed, far too little appreciative of the freedom he has, and far too prone to flee from hard work to the solace of the martyr's shroud. When I first began practise as a critic, in 1908, there was yet plenty of excuse for putting it on. It was a time of almost incon-ceivable complacency and conformity. Hamilton Wright Mabie was still alive and still taken seriously, and all the young pedagogues who aspired to the critical gown imitated him in his watchful stupidity. This camorra had delivered a violent wallop to Theodore Dreiser eight years before, and he was yet suffering from his bruises; it was not until 1911 that he printed "Jennie Gerhardt." Miss Harriet Mon-roe and her gang of new poets were still dispersed and inarticulate; Miss Amy Lowell, as yet unaware of Imagism, was writing polite doggerel in the man-ner of a New England schoolmarm; the reigning dramatists of the nation were Augustus Thomas, David Belasco and Clyde Fitch; Miss Cather was imitating Mrs. Wharton; Hergesheimer had six years to go before he'd come to "The Lay Anthony"; Cabell was known only as one who provided the text for illustrated gift-books; the American novelists most admired by most publishers, by most readers and by all practising critics were Richard Harding Davis, Robert W. Chambers and James Lane Allen. It is hard indeed, in retrospect, to picture those remote days just as they were. They seem almost fabulous. The chief critical organ of the Republic was actually the Literary Supplement of the New York *Times*. The *Dial* was down with diabetes in Chicago; the *Nation* was made dreadful by the gloomy humors of Paul Elmer More; the *Bookman* was even more saccharine and sophomoric than it is today. When the mild and *pianissimo* revolt of the middle 90's—a feeble echo of the English revolt—had spent itself, the Presbyterians marched in and took possession of the works. Most of the erstwhile revoltés boldly took the veil—notably Hamlin Garland. No novel that told the truth about life as Americans were living it, no poem that departed from the old patterns, no play that had the merest ghost of an idea in it had a chance. When, in 1908, Mrs. Mary Roberts Rinehart printed a conventional mystery story which yet managed to have a trace of sense in it, it caused a sensation. And when, two years later, Dr. William Lyon Phelps printed a book of criticism in which he actually ranked Mark Twain alongside Emerson and Hawthorne, there was as great a stirring beneath the college elms as if a naked fancy woman had run across the campus. If Hergesheimer had come into New York in 1908 with "Cytherea" under his arm, he would have worn out his pantaloons on publishers' benches without getting so much as a polite kick. If Eugene O'Neill had come to Broadway with "The Hairy Ape," he would have been sent to Edward E. Rose to learn the elements of his trade. The devilish and advanced thing, in those days, was for the fat lady star to give a couple of matinées of Ibsen's "A Doll's House."

A great many men and a few women addressed themselves to the dispersal of this fog. Some of them were imaginative writers who found it simply impossible to bring themselves within the prevailing rules; some were critics; others were young publishers. As I look back, I can't find any sign of concerted effort; it was, in the main, a case of each on his own. The more contumacious of the younger critics, true enough, tended to rally 'round Huneker, who, as a matter of fact, was very little interested in American letters, and the young novelists had a leader in Dreiser, who, I suspect, was quite unaware of most of them. However, it was probably Dreiser who chiefly gave form to the movement, despite the fact that for eleven long years he was silent. Not only was there a useful rallying-point in the idiotic suppression of "Sister Carrie"; there was also the encouraging fact of the man's massive immovability. Physically and mentally he loomed up like a sort of headland—a great crag of basalt that no conceivable assault seemed able to touch. His predecessor, Frank Norris, was of much softer stuff. Norris, had he lived longer, would have been wooed and ruined, I fear, by the Mabies, Boyntons and other such Christian critics, as Garland had been wooed and ruined before him. Dreiser, fortunately for American letters, never had to face any such seduction. The critical schoolmarms, young and old, fell upon him with violence the moment he appeared above the horizon of his native steppe, and soon he was the storm center of a battle-royal that lasted nearly twenty years. The man himself was solid, granitic, without nerves. Very little cunning was in him and not much bellicose enterprise, but he showed a truly appalling tenacity. The pedagogues tried to scare him to death, they tried to stampede his partisans and they tried to put him into Coventry and get him forgotten, but they failed every time. The more he was reviled, sneered at, neglected, the more resolutely he stuck to his formula. That formula is now every serious American novelist's formula. They all try to write better than Dreiser, and not a few of them succeed, but they all follow him in his fundamental purpose—to make the novel true. Dreiser added something, and here following him is harder: he tried to make the novel poignant—to add sympathy, feeling, imagination to understanding. It will be a long while before that enterprise is better managed than he managed it in "Jennie Gerhardt."

Today, it seems to me, the American imaginative writer, whether he be novelist, poet or dramatist, is quite as free as he deserves to be. He is free to depict the life about him precisely as he sees it, and to interpret it in any manner he pleases. The publishers of the land, once so fearful of novelty, are now so hospitable to it that they constantly fail to distinguish the novelty that has hard thought behind it from that which has only some Village mountebank's desire to stagger the wives of Rotarians. Our stage is perhaps the freest in the world—not only to sensations, but also to ideas. Our poets get into print regularly with stuff so bizarre and unearthly that only Christian Scientists can understand it. The extent of this new freedom, indeed, is so great that large numbers of persons appear to be unable to believe in it; they are constantly getting into sweats about the taboos and inhibitions that remain, for example, those nourished by comstockery. But the importance and puissance of comstockery, I believe, is quite as much overestimated as the importance and puissance of the objurgations still hurled at sense and honesty by the provincial professors of American Idealism, the Genius of America, and other such

phantasms.   The Comstocks, true enough, still raid
an occasional book, particularly when their funds are
running low and there is need to inflame Christian
men, but that their monkeyshines ever actually *suppress* a book of any consequence I very much doubt.
The flood is too vast for them.   Chasing a minnow
with desperate passion, they let a whole school of
whales go by.   In any case, they confine their operations to the single field of sex, and it must be plain
that it is not in the field of sex that the hottest battles
against the old American manner have been fought
and won.   "Three Soldiers" was far more subversive
of that manner than all the stories of sex ever written
in America—and yet "Three Soldiers" came out with
the imprint of one of the most respectable of American publishers, and was scarcely challenged.   "Babbitt" scored a victory that was still easier, and yet
more significant, for its target was the double one
of American business and American Christianity; it
set the whole world to laughing at two things that are
far more venerated in the United States than the
bodily chastity of women.   Nevertheless, "Babbitt"
went down so easily that even the alfalfa *Gelehrten*
joined in whooping for it, apparently on the theory
that praising Lewis would make the young of the
national species forget Dreiser.   Victimized by their
own craft, the *Gelehrten* thus made a foul attack upon
their own principles, for if their principles did not

stand against just such anarchistic and sacrilegious books, then they were without any sense whatever, as was and is, indeed, the case.

I shall not rehearse the steps in the advance from "Sister Carrie," suppressed and proscribed, to "Babbitt," swallowed and hailed. The important thing is that, despite the caterwauling of the Comstocks and the pedagogues, a reasonable freedom for the serious artist now prevails—that publishers stand ready to print him, that critics exist who are competent to recognize him and willing to do battle for him, and that there is a large public eager to read him. What use is he making of his opportunity? Certainly not the worst use possible, but also certainly not the best. He is free, but he is not yet, perhaps, worthy of freedom. He lets the popular magazine, the movie and the cheap-John publisher pull him too hard in one direction; he lets the vagaries of his politics pull him too hard in another. Back in 1908 I predicted the destruction of Upton Sinclair the artist by Upton Sinclair the visionary and reformer. Sinclair's bones now bleach upon the beach. Beside them repose those of many another man and woman of great promise—for example, Winston Churchill. Floyd Dell is on his way—one novel and two doses of Greenwich Village psychology. Hergesheimer writes novelettes for the *Saturday Evening Post*. Willa Cather has won the

Pulitzer Prize—a transaction comparable to the election of Charles W. Eliot to the Elks.   Masters turns to prose that somehow fails to come off.   Dreiser, forgetting his trilogy, experiments rather futilely with the drama, the essay, free verse.   Fuller renounces the novel for book reviewing.   Tarkington is another Pulitzer prizeman, always on the verge of first-rate work but always falling short by an inch. Many of the White Hopes of ten or fifteen years ago perished in the war, as surely victims of its slaughter as Rupert Brook or Otto Braun; it is, indeed, curious to note that practically every American author who moaned and sobbed for democracy between the years 1914 and 1919 is now extinct.   The rest have gone down the chute of the movies.

But all this, after all, may signify little.   The shock troops have been piled up in great masses, but the ground is cleared for those that follow.   Well, then, what of the youngsters?   Do they show any sign of seizing their chance?   The answer is yes and no.   On the one hand there is a group which, revolving 'round the *Bookman,* talks a great deal and accomplishes nothing.   On the other hand there is a group which, revolving 'round the *Dial* and the *Little Review,* talks even more and does even less. But on the third hand, as it were, there is a group which says little and saws wood.   There seems to be little in common between its members, no sign of a formal movement, with its *blague* and its bombast, but all of them have this in common: that they owe both their opportunity and their method to the revolution that followed "Sister Carrie." Most of them are from the Middle West, but they are distinct from the Chicago crowd, now degenerated to posturing and worse. They are sophisticated, disillusioned, free from cant, and yet they have imagination. The raucous protests of the evangelists of American Idealism seem to have no more effect upon them than the advances of the Expressionists, Dadaists and other such café-table prophets. Out of this dispersed and ill-defined group, I believe, something will come. Its members are those who are free from the two great delusions which, from the beginning, have always cursed American letters: the delusion that a work of art is primarily a moral document, that its purpose is to make men better Christians and more docile cannon-fodder, and the delusion that it is an exercise in logic, that its purpose is to prove something. These delusions, lingering beyond their time, are responsible for most of the disasters visible in the national literature today—the disasters of the radicals as well as those of the 100 per cent. dunderheads. The writers of the future, I hope and believe, will carefully avoid both of them.

XVII. PEOPLE AND THINGS

1

The Capital of a Great Republic

THE fourth secretary of the Paraguayan legation. . . . The chief clerk to the House committee on industrial arts and expositions. . . .
The secretary to the secretary to the Secretary of
Labor. . . . The brother to the former Congressman
from the third Idaho district. . . . The messenger to
the chief of the Senate folding-room. . . . The doorkeeper outside the committee-room of the House committee on the disposition of useless executive papers.
. . . The chief correspondent of the Toomsboro,
Ga., *Banner* in the Senate press-gallery. . . . The
stenographer to the assistant chief entomologist of
the Bureau of Animal Industry. . . . The third assistant chief computor in the office of the Naval
Almanac. . . . The assistant Attorney-General in
charge of the investigation of postal frauds in the
South Central States. . . . The former wife of the
former secretary to the former member of the Interstate Commerce Commission. . . . The brother to

the wife of the *chargé d'affaires* of Czecho-Slovakia.
. . . The bootlegger to the ranking Democratic member of the committee on the election of President, Vice-President and representatives in Congress. . . . The acting assistant doorkeeper of the House visitors' gallery. . . . The junior Senator from Delaware. . . . The assistant to the secretary to the chief clerk of the Division of Audits and Disbursements, Bureau of Stationary and Supplies, Postoffice Department. . . . The press-agent to the chaplain of the House. . . . The commercial attaché to the American legation at Quito. . . . The chauffeur to the fourth assistant Postmaster-General. . . . The acting substitute elevator-man in the Washington monument. . . . The brother to the wife of the brother-in-law of the Vice-President. . . . The aunt to the sister of the wife of the officer in charge of ceremonials, State Department. . . . The neighbor of the cousin of the step-father of the sister-in-law of the President's pastor. . . . The superintendent of charwomen in Temporary Storehouse B7, Bureau of Navy Yards and Docks. . . . The assistant confidential clerk to the chief clerk to the acting chief examiner of the Patent Office. . . . The valet to the Chief Justice.

2

Ambassadors of Christ

Fifth avenue rectors with shining morning faces, preaching on Easter to pews packed with stock-brokers, defendants in salacious divorce suits, members of the Sulgrave Foundation and former Zionists. . . . Evangelists of strange, incomprehensible cults whooping and bawling at two or three half-witted old women and half a dozen scared little girls in corrugated iron tabernacles down near the railroad-yards. . . . Mormon missionaries pulling door-bells in Wheeling, W. Va., and Little Rock, Ark., and handing naughty-looking tracts to giggling servant girls. . . . Baptist doctors of divinity calling upon John the Baptist and John D. Rockefeller to bear witness that the unducked will sweat in hell forever-more. . . . Methodist candidates for the sacred frock, sent out to preach trial sermons to backward churches in the mail-order belt, proving magnificently in one hour that Darwin was an ignoramus and Huxley a scoundrel. . . . Irish priests denouncing the Ku Klux Klan. . . . Rabbis denouncing Henry Ford. . . . Presbyterians denouncing Flo Ziegfeld. . . . Fashionable divines officiating at gaudy home weddings, their ears alert for the popping of corks. . . . Street evangelists in Zanesville, O., trying to convince a cop and five newsboys that no man will be saved unless he be born again. . . . Missionaries in smelly gospel-shops along the waterfront, expounding the doctrine of the atonement to boozy Norwegian sailors, half of them sound asleep. . . . Cadaverous high-church Episcopalians. . . . Little fat Lutherans with the air of prosperous cheese-mongers. . . . Dunkards with celluloid collars and no neckties. . . . Southern Methodists who still believe in slavery. . . . Former plumbers, threshing-machine engineers and horse-doctors turned into United Brethren bishops. . . . Missionaries collecting money from the mill children in Raleigh, N. C., to convert the Spaniards and Italians to Calvinism. . . . Episcopal archdeacons cultivating the broad English *a.* . . . Swedenborgians trying to explain the "Arcana Cœlestia" to flabbergasted newspaper reporters. . . . Polish clergymen leaping out of the windows at Polish weddings in Johnstown, Pa., hoping that the next half-dozen beer-bottles won't hit them. . . . Methodists pulling wires for bishoprics. . . . Quakers foreclosing mortgages. . . . Baptists busy among the women.

3

Bilder aus schöner Zeit

The excellent lunch that the illustrious Crispi used to serve at Delmonico's at five o'clock in the afternoon. . . . The incomparable orange blossom cocktails at Sherry's, and the plates of salted nuts. . . . The tavern cocktails at the Beaux Arts, each with its dash of absinthe. . . . The Franziskaner Mai-Bock at Lüchow's. . . . Dear old Sieg's noble Rhine wines at the Kaiserhof. . . . The long-tailed clams and Spring onions at Rogers', with Pilsner to wash them down. . . . The amazingly good American quasi-Pilsner, made by Herr Abner, on the Raleigh roof in Washington. . . . The Castel del Remy at the Brevoort, cheap but perfect. . . . The very dark Kulmbacher at the Pabst place in 125th street in the last days of civilization. . . . The burgundy from the Cresta Blanca vineyards in California. . . . Michelob on warm Summer evenings, with the crowd singing "Throw Out the Lifeline!" . . . The old-time Florestan cocktails—50 per cent. London gin, 25 per cent. French vermouth and 25 per cent. Martini-Rossi, with a dash of Angostura bitters—drink half, then drink a glass of beer, and then drink the other half. . . . That Hoboken red wine, so strangely smooth and lovely. . . . The bad red wine (but capital cooking) at the Frenchman's in Lexington avenue. . . . Del Pezzo's superb Chianti. . . . The ale at Keen's. . . . Obst's herrings, with Löwenbraü to slack them. . . . The astounding cocktail made by the head waiter at Henri's. . . . Drinking Faust all night in St. Louis in 1904. . . . The musty

ale at Losekam's in Washington. . . . The draft
Helles at Krüger's in Philadelphia. . . . A Pilsner
luncheon at the old Grand Union, from one to six.
. . . A stray bottle of perfect sauterne found in Rah-
way, New Jersey. . . . A wild night drinking Swed-
ish punch and hot water. . . . Two or three hot
Scotch nights. . . . Twenty or thirty Bass' ale nights.
. . . Five or six hundred Pilsner nights. . . .

4

The High Seas

The kid who sits in the bucket of tar. . . . The
buxom stewardess who comes in and inquires archly
if one rang. . . . The humorous piano-tuner who
tunes the grand piano in the music-room in the 15-
16ths-tone scale. . . . The electric fan which, when
a stray zephyr blows in through the porthole, makes
a noise like a dentist's drill. . . . The alien ship's
printer who, in the daily wireless paper, reports a
baseball score of 165 to 3. . . . The free Christian
Science literature in the reading-room. . . . The
pens in the writing-room. . . . The elderly *Gross-
händler* with the young wife. . . . The red-haired
girl in the green sweater. . . . The retired bootlegger disguised as a stockbroker. . . . The stockbroker disguised as a United States Senator. . . .

The boy who climbs into the lifeboat. . . . The chief steward wearing the No. 18¾ collar. . . . The mysterious pipes that run along the stateroom ceilings. . . . The discovery that one forgot to pack enough undershirts. . . . The night watchman who raps on the door at 3.30 A. M. to deliver a wireless message reading "Sorry missed you. Bon voyage". . . The bartender who adds a dash of witchhazel to cocktails. . . . The wilting flowers standing in ice-pitchers and spittoons in the hallways. . . . The fight in the steerage. . . . The old lady who gets stewed and sends for the doctor. . . . The news that the ship is in Long. 43°, 41′, 16″ W, Lat. 40°, 23′, 39″ N. . . . The report that the starboard propeller has lost a blade.

5

The Shrine of Mnemosyne

The little town of Kirkwall, in the Orkney Islands, in a mid-Winter mist, flat and charming like a Japanese print. . . . San Francisco and the Golden Gate from the top of Twin Peaks. . . . Gibraltar on a Spring day, all in pastel shades, like the back-drop for a musical comedy. . . . My first view of the tropics, the palm-trees suddenly bulging out of the darkness of dawn, the tremendous stillness, the

sweetly acid smell, the immeasurable strangeness.
. . . The Trentino on a glorious morning, up from
Verona to the Brenner Pass. . . . Central Germany
from Bremen to Munich, all in one day, with the
apple trees in bloom. . . . Copenhagen on a wild
night, with the *Polizei* combing the town for the
American who upset the piano. . . . Christiania in
January, with the snow-clad statue of Ibsen looming
through the gloom like a ghost in a cellar. . . . The
beach at Tybee Island, with the faint, blood-curdling
rattle of the land-crabs. . . . Jacksonville after the
fire in 1902, with the hick militiamen firing their
machine-guns all night. . . . The first inauguration
of Woodrow, and the pretty suffragette who drank
beer with me at the Raleigh. . . . A child playing
in the yard of a God-forsaken town in the Wyoming
desert. . . . Bryan's farewell speech at the St. Louis
Convention in 1904. . . . Hampton Court on Chest-
nut Sunday. . . . A New Year's Eve party on a
Danish ship, 500 miles off the coast of Greenland.
. . . The little pile of stones on the beach of Wat-
ling's Island, marking the place where Columbus
landed. . . . The moon of the Caribbees, seen from
a 1000-ton British tramp. . . . A dull night in a
Buffalo hotel, reading the American Revised Version
of the New Testament. . . . The day I received the
proofs of my first book. . . . A good-bye on an Hoboken pier. . . . The Palace Hotel in Madrid.

INDEX